Temple and Shrine Treasures
in the
Custody of the Kyoto National Museum

This book was made possible
by a grant from the Toshiba International Foundation

Temple and Shrine Treasures
in the
Custody of the Kyoto National Museum

Temple and Shrine Treasures in the
Custody of the Kyoto National Museum
Published by
Kyoto National Museum
Produced by
Otsuka Kogeisha Co., Ltd.
Printed in Japan.
© KYOTO NATIONAL MUSEUM, 1992

INDEX

Greetings

Masterpieces of Kyoto National Museum was published last year for the convenience of our visitors and has enjoyed a favorable receptions. This time, *Temple and Shrine Treasures in the Custody of the Kyoto National Museum* is published, featuring the most excellent items among the art objects entrusted to our museum by temples and shrines. Visitors surveying the ordinary exhibition of our museum may realize that many of the exhibits are not museum collections but temples' and shrines' treasures entrusted to our museum. This is due to the social circumstances of the days when our museum was established and due to the purpose for which it was established.

The Kyoto National Museum was officially established in 1889 through the announcement of the Minister of the Imperial Household. It was the period of strong westernization trends, which began with the Meiji Restoration and the anti-Buddhist movement. Historical cultural properties, which had been kept in old temples and shrines in Kyoto and Nara, were neglected and their proper maintenance was difficult. According to a well-known anecdote, the five-storied pagoda of Kōfuku-ji temple in Nara was put on sale, but nobody wanted to buy it because disassembling it was expensive. Most of the Japanese art objects in Boston Museum, which are said to number more than 50,000, were acquired during that period by Fenollosa, Bigelow, and Tenshin Okakura. The flow of cultural properties out of the country could not be stopped.

Under those circumstances, our museum was opened in 1897 as the "Imperial Museum of Kyoto" for the purpose of collecting and protecting the treasures of temples and shrines in Kyoto and the surrounding Kinki area. Our museum now can look back on a history of one hundred years, although between 1924 and 1952 it was administered by the City of Kyoto as "Imperial Gift, Kyoto Museum". During that period everything had to be sacrificed for World War II, which came to an end with a miserable result, followed by chaotic social conditions. The basic activity of a museum — collecting objects — had been discontinued.

The year 1952 marked a new beginning for our museum as the "Kyoto National Museum". The numbers of temples' and shrines' treasures that were in our museum's custody in 1952 and in 1990 are shown in the following chart.

	painting	calligraphy	sculpture	architecture	ceramics
1924	600	385	93	2	45
1990	656	458	114	1	36

	textile art	lacquered art	metal work	archaeology	history	total
1924	63	42	33	38	42	1343
1990	90	103	67	72	18	1615

There were slight changes in each category, but the number of temples' and shrines' treasures in our custody keeps increasing through the addition of objects found during excavations and other discoveries. Although the total number of temple and shrine objects in our custody is not as large as the number of objects in the museum collections, which is 4,556, or the number of objects from private collections entrusted to our museum, which count 3,934, the temple and shrine objects are superior in quality. The number of objects registered as National Treasures or Cultural Properties by the government is about 150 for the museum collections, while an amazingly high number of 550 items of temples' and shrines' treasures are registered; this is almost one third of the total number of entrusted objects. The high quality of the art objects selected for this catalogue is obvious and it nees no mention that they form the nucleus of our ordinary exhibition.

The ordinary exhibition in the New Exhibition building, which was established in 1966, consists of archaeological objects, ceramics and sculptures on the first floor, and paintings, calligraphic pieces, textile art, lacquered works, and metalworks on the second floor. These exhibits are displayed in such a way that an overview of Japanese art (including Chinese and Korean art, which excerted great influence on Japanese art) can be obtained by walking through all the rooms. The exhibits are replaced monthly, or in some categories every three months, or from time to time for conservation purpose. Principally, art objects made of rather fragile materials, such as paintings, calligraphic works and textile art, are not on display for more than 30 days a year. Nonetheless, the overall view of Japanese art-history is still observable. The art objects selected for this catalogue are expected to be on display during the high seasons mainly — which are spring and autumn. We hope that this catalogue will serve as a reference for visitors of our museum.

We selected only 135 items for this catalogue because of a limit on the number of pages, but in fact all 1615 temple and shrine treasures are equally valued and displayed at the ordinary exhibition. Six items, which are not in our custody, are included in this catalogue because we wanted to organize it as a self-contained book on Japanese art history, and we express our sincere appreciation to the owners of those art objects.

Most of the explanations of exhibition rooms 1 to 16 were duplicated from those printed in *Masterpieces of Kyoto National Museum*.

ROOM 1

This room covers excavated items from the Paleolithic Age (more than 30,000 years ago), when people started to live in this country, to the Tumulus Age (about 300~710A.D.), when the unification of the country began.

In the Paleolithic Age, earthenware was not yet made, and the main excavated items are chipped stone tools. They look simple, but basic manufacturing standards can be observed, according to the areas and ages.

In the Jōmon period (ca10,000~ca300B.C.), strong and aesthetically pleasing earthenware was made. We can imagine the lives of our unknown ancestors through such items. Other exhibits of this period are tools for hunting, prayer and imprecation.

In the Yayoi period (ca300B.C~ca300A.D.), rice cultivation was introduced, small villages, which were called "Kuni", were formed, and wars started. Arrows, which were used only for hunting in the previous era, were targeted on human beings as enemies, and the worship of bronze and iron weapons led people to make weapon-shaped ritual implements such as bronze halberds and swords.

In the Tumulus period, powerful leaders constructed their gigantic tumuli. Several objects were buried with bodies, including mirrors and special stones which were given to the local leaders from the central administrator.

As a supplement to the exhibits, photographs of excavating sites are displayed.

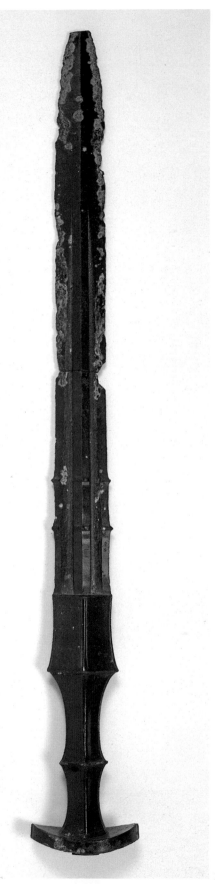

1

1
Bronze Sword with a Hilt.

Length: 51.5cm.
Middle Yayoi period 1st century B.C.
Excavated from the jar-type coffin No.1 in
Mikumo Minamikōji, Itoshima county,
Fukushima prefecture.
Shōfuku-ji temple, Fukushima.
Important Cultural Property.

A jar-type coffin, which was assumed to be the coffin of the King of Inanokuni of the Yayoi period, was excavated in 1822 in Mikumo Minamikōji, Maehara-chō, Itoshima county in Fukushima prefecture. Many objects, such as thirty-five bronze mirrors, bronze swords, bronze halberds, glassware, and *magatama* jewelry, were within and alongside the coffin as burial accessories. One of the most notable objects is this sword. It is said to have been made in Japan, modeled after a slim bronze sword from Korea. Usually, hilts were separately made of wood and attached to swords, but this sword is different. The hilt was cast together with the blade, which is a rare method of manufacturing swords. Because the metalic material used is bronze with plenty of tin, this sword must have been glittering in a silver color. This sword was a suitable object to express the dignity of the king.

2
Dōtaku Bronze Bell with a Tossen Type Handle and Keça-dasuki Pattern.

Height: 107.0cm.
Late Yayoi period, 3rd century A.D.
Excavated from Bikunijō, Yosa county,
Kyoto prefecture.
Bairin-ji temple, Kyoto.
Important Cultural Property.

This bell was reportedly excavated from Bikunijō near Bairin-ji temple during the Edo period. *Dōtaku* bronze bells are classified chronologically into four groups according to the styles of their handles: The handles, which were added originally for the purpose of suspending the bell, became less functional and more ornamental in later years. This bronze bell belongs to the latest group called *Tossen*-type bells. Within the *Tossen*-type group, it is classified as type 5, which is the latest one. Bells of this type were large and often more than one meter high. The bodies of the bells were decorated with vertical and horizontal thick lines, the so-called "Tossen" lines. This bell in Bairin-ji temple, which has been preserved in better condition than other bells of the same type, is a very important object for studying the casting techniques of those days.

►

ROOM 2

This room covers archaeological items of the Nara period (710~794) and Heian period (794~1185), including roof tiles, excavated from the site of Heian-kyō (today's Kyoto) which was the capital for about one thousand years.

Tiles with Buddhist figures used as ornaments for the temples in the Hakuhō cultural period (ca650~710), cinerary urns and records of the dead which indicate the custom of cremation in the Nara period are also exhibited.

In the Heian period, there was an attempt to identify Shintō gods and Buddhist figures and several pendent God-Buddha amulets were made. There also was a belief in the approach of doomsday. Seeking salvation, people copied sutras and buried them in sutra mounds. Among the excavated objects from such mounds there are many excellent metalworks which help us to comprehend the culture of the Heian period. Not only the artistic achievement but also the people's life of those days can be observed through these exhibits.

3
Reliquary and Ornaments.

Excavated at Nagao, Shigasato-chō,
Ōtsu city.
Height of the Reliquary: 3cm.
Asuka period, late 7th century.
Ōmi shrine, Shiga.
National Treasure.

Sūfuku-ji temple was built as a guardian temple of the Capital Ōtsu-kyō during the reign of Emperor Tenchi. Three pagodas were constructed on the three hills separated by the streams. When the sites of the pagodas were excavated in 1938, this reliquary and its containers and accompanying ornaments were recovered from the cavity of the central foundation of one of the stupas. The reliquary was made of green glass with a metalic lid, and three crystal balls were kept in it. The reliquary was contained in three containers made of gold, silver and gilt-bronze, which were inserted into one another in this order. The accompanying ornaments were an amethyst jewel, a glass bead, a jade bead, a silver coin, an iron mirror with gilt-bronze back, and a bronze bell.

6

5

14

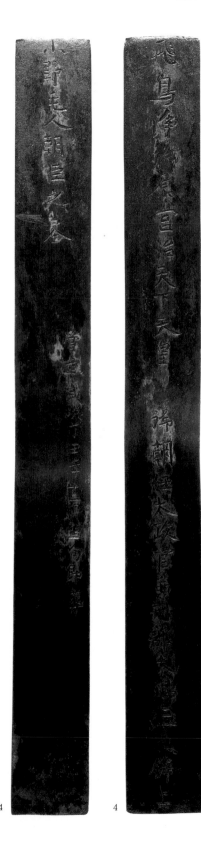

6
Gilt-bronze Cinerary Container
for Ina-no-Ōmura's Ash.

Height: 24.2cm.
Excavated from Kashiba-chō, Kita
Katsuragi county, Nara prefecture.
Asuka period, dated 707.
Shitennō-ji temple, Osaka.
National Treasure.

This cinerary container was excavated from underneath a jar, which was placed upside down, during the Meiwa era (1764–1772) in the Edo period. The shape of this container is unique: It is a sphere which consists of a hemispheric body and a hemispheric lid. There is a similar example reportedly excavated in Saga prefecture, but it does not bear an inscription. This container for Ina-no-Ōmura's ash bears an inscription of 319 letters in thirty-nine lines on the surface of the lid. According to the inscription, Ino-no-Ōmura was a descendant of the Emperor Senka and began his career as an official during the reign of Emperor Jitō. Later, he served with Emperor Mommu as a "Shōnagon" official, and when the law of "Taihōrei" was established, he gained the title "Jūgo-i" and became a member of the aristocracy. He was appointed feudal lord of Echigo province in 705 and died there in 707. It is also recorded that he was buried in his birth place, Yamakimi-no-sato of Katsuragishita county in Yamato, which is today's Kashiba-chō, Kitakatsuragi county in Nara.

4   ▶
Gilt-bronze Memorial Tablet of
Ono-no-Emishi.

Length: 58.9cm, Width: 5.8cm.
Excavated at Kamitakano, Sakyō-ku,
Kyoto city.
Nara period, early 8th century.
Sudo shrine, Kyoto.
National Treasure.

When an old grave was excavated at today's Kamitakano, Sakyō-ku in Kyoto city in 1613, this memorial tablet of Ono-no-Emishi was found. This excavated tablet had once been returned to the grave, but since the grave was robbed during the Meiji period, it was finally taken out again in 1914 for the purpose of preservation. It is a cast bronze tablet, which was coated with gold after the record had been engraved on both sides. On the front side, Ono-no-Emishi's career is recorded: He was serving with Emperor Temmu as an official "Nagon", equivalent to the later "Shō-fourth class" official of the Ministry of "Osakabe". The inscription on the backside says that the grave is Ono-no-Emishi's and gives the date of his burial. However, this Memorial tablet was made during the Nara period, which was later than his death. Ono-no-Emishi is a son of Ono-no-Imoko, who as a well-known envoy was sent to China during the Sui dynasty. Nothing else than what is written on the memorial tablet is known about him.

5
Tile with Design of an Angel.

Size: 39 × 39 × 8cm.
Excavated at Oka, Asuka village, Takaichi
county in Nara prefecture.
Asuka period, late 7th century.
Oka-dera temple, Nara.
Important Cultural Property.

The flat surface of this tile is almost square. An illustration is on one side with a plain 3.8cm wide edging along its rim. The figure of a kneeling angel holding a holy cloth and looking upward to the heaven is carved in relief within the edging. The drapery is waving in the wind gracefully. Some part of the angel's hair is sticking up while other parts are hanging down, which may indicate that this figure has just arrived after descending from Heaven. There are few examples of illustrated tiles in Japan; a tile with a phoenix illustration reportedly excavated at Oka-dera temple is one of them. It is assumed that this tile was made under the influence of Korean tiles. It might have been attached to the side of the *Shumidan* platform of the main Buddhist statue of the temple.

4   4

7
Gilt-bronze Cylindrical Sutra
Case of Fujiwara Michinaga.

Height: 36.1cm, Bottom diameter: 16.1cm.
Excavated from the Kimpusen sutra
mound, Yoshino county in Nara prefecture.
Late Heian period, dated 1007.
Kimpu shrine, Nara.
National Treasure.

This is the sutra case buried by Fujiwara Michinaga in August 1007 when he was a minister, a so-called "Sa-daijin". The case is cylindrical, and four small holes are near its mouth, through which nails were hammered in to fasten the lid. An inscription of 511 letters is written on the body of the cylinder in 24 lines, which says that the enclosed *Hokekyō* sutra and fifteen volumes of other Buddhist sutras were copied by Michinaga himself. The inscription also contains Michinaga's petition: "May I repay Shaka's (Buddha's) grace, enjoy Miroku's (Maitreya's) favor, and get acquainted with Zaō!", and, "May I be calm and offer prayers to Amida (Amitabha) at my death and go to Heaven!". It was a common wish among the aristocrats in the Heian period to die when Miroku emerges. It indicates their attachment to life and their wish for a peaceful life in Heaven.

8
Gilt-bronze Sutra Case.

Total height: 24.2cm,
Case: 33.5 × 17.0 × 12.3cm.
Excavated from the Kimpusen sutra
mound in Yoshino county, Nara prefecture.
Late Heian period, 11th century.
Kimpusen-ji temple, Nara.
National Treasure.

This sutra case is accompanied by a case-stand with *Sagi-ashi* type legs, and both the case and the stand are gilded. The gilded area of the case is the entire outer surface including the bottom and some part of the inner surface, which is where the cap covers the case. The sutra case is made in rectangular *Inrō-buta-zukuri* style with the corners of the case in *Irikuma* style. The top of the cap is slightly rising and the rim is made in *Fukurin* style. The place of the case-stand is made so as to match the shape of the case. Legs are fastened to the four corners of this plate. The sutra mound on Mt. Kimpusen became popular among aristocrats since Fujiwara Michinaga climbed up and buried sutras there by himself. Because this sutra case is such an excellent piece, it possibly was buried by some high-ranked aristocrat. Since Fujiwara Moromichi visited Mt. Kimpusen for the second time in August, 1090, some historians assume that it was this very sutra case which was buried on that occasion.

(The surface of the mirror)

9
Mirror with Line-engraved Amitabha Triad and Twelve Buddhist Figures.

Front Diameter: 14.5cm,
Back Diameter: 14.1cm.
Late Heian period, 11th century.
Rinnō-ji temple, Tochigi.
Important Cultural Property.

The style of mirrors, whose characteristic is line-engraved Buddhist or Shintoist figures on the front surface, was developed on the basis of the idea of "Honji-suijaku-setsu", which expounded the correspondence between Buddhist and Shintoist deities. This is an eight-foliate cast nickel mirror with decoration of clouds and two pairs of phoenixes. On the front surface, Amida-sanzon (Amitābha triad) and twelve Buddhist figures, which represent light, are engraved in lines. The surface of the mirror is slightly curved, and the figure of Amitābha, seated cross-legged on a lotus leaf with his hands in the "Jōin" meditative position, is represented in the center. The attendants are depicted on both sides of Amitābha, and the twelve figures are placed around the triad on flying clouds. The carving techniques used for this mirror are hairlike line-engraving and needle hammering. The engravings were done carefully.

10
Small Bronze Pagoda

Height: 55.2cm.
Excavated from the Kurama-dera sutra
mound in Kurama Honmachi, Sakyō-ku,
Kyoto.
Late Heian period, 12th century.
Kurama-dera temple, Kyoto.
National Treasure.

Many buried objects have been excavated from the Kurama-dera sutra mound since the Meiji period. This small pagoda is the container of a Buddhist sutra to be buried underground. It is made of cast bronze and consists of a foundation, the body, the roof, and the top, which were made separately. The foundation is of "Dansei-tsumi Kidan" type. The sides of the foundation are divided into two sections, both of which are decorated. The body, which has the shape of a short bottle, is placed on a lotus seat. The roof is pyramidal and roof tiles are depicted. The round tiles are described carefully even down to their joints, whereas the joints of the flat tiles are not depicted. The back of the eaves is flat, but the end of the eaves is slightly curving upward.

ROOM 3

Chinese and Korean ceramics are exhibited in this room, showing the dates and categories.

The earliest Chinese ceramics are colored ware and unpainted earthenware in the Pre-dynastic Age (2000~1000B.C.). These are followed by pottery of the Dynastic periods, which include the objects buried with bodies in tumuli in the Yin and Zhou dynasties, the Period of Warring States, Han dynasty, the Period of six dynasties, Sui and Tang dynasties. Among them, a green-glazed ducks' pond in the Han dynasty, warriors' figures in the Period of six dynasties (3rd~6th century), a lady holding a dog in the Tang dynasty (7th~9th century), three-color-glazed figures for burial are outstanding. Chinese ceramic art has made remarkable progress since the Song dynasty (10th~12th century) when celadon, white celadon, black celadon and Ci-zhou pottery were manufactured. In the Yuan dynasty (13th~14th century) blue-flower porcelain and five-colored porcelain came to be the main stream. The development of Chinese ceramics until the Qing dynasty (17th~20th century) is displayed, showing the chronological order and categories.

The Korean ceramics collection covers celadon, damascened celadon, white celadon, blue flower porcelain, iron-coated ware in the Yi dynasty (1392~1910).

11
***Celadon and White Porcelain
Containers of the Gōsu Type.***
**Esshū (Yue-zhou) kiln and Northern
kiln in China.**

Large celadon
Height: 12.0cm, Mouth Diameter: 17.4cm,
Bottom Diameter: 8.4cm.
Small celadon
Height: 7.8cm, Mouth Diameter: 9.1cm,
Bottom Diameter: 4.4cm.
White porcelain
Height: 4.0cm, Mouth Diameter: 4.8cm,
Bottom Diameter: 2.6cm.
Tang dynasty, 9th century.
Ninna-ji temple, Kyoto.
Important Cultural Property.

A set of *Gōsu* type containers was excavated in 1915 from the site of the Endō Hall within the compound of Ninna-ji temple. Two of the containers were made of celadon, one was white porcelain, one was gold, and one was silver (later stolen). The containers shown here are from that set. The celadon containers are assumed to have been made in the Esshū (Yue-zhou) kiln in Zhe-jian province, and the white porcelain container is assumed to have been made in the Hwabei northern district. They were made during the late 9th century in the Tang dynasty. They are notable as reliable research materials, excavated in Japan.

12
Temmoku Type Tea Bowl with Furnace-Transmuted Glazing.
Ken (Jian) kiln in China.

Height: 6.4cm, Mouth Diameter: 12.2cm,
Foot Diameter: 3.4cm.
Southern Song dynasty, 12th–13th
centuries.
Ryūkō-in temple, Kyoto.
National Treasure.

This tea bowl is thought to be the most attractive piece among the *Temmoku* type tea bowls made in the Ken (Jian) kiln in Fujian province. An old document, "Kundaikan Sōchō-ki", written during the Muromachi period, says: "Furnace-transmuted glaze is the most splendid product of the Ken kiln. There is nothing in this world that surpasses this glaze. The background color is truly black, and small mottles of dark and light lapis lazuli color are sprinkled over it ....". This bowl is well known as one of the three rare masterpieces with furnace-transmuted glaze; the other two are the *Inaba Temmoku* bowls kept in the Seikadō Bunko and the Fujita Art Museum. All three masterpieces have been kept in Japan. This bowl was originally owned by the Tennōji-ya, Tsuda family, wealthy merchants in Sakai. It is reported that since the foundation of Tsuda Sōkyū's family temple, Daitsū-an, the bowl had been kept there as a temple treasure until Tsuda Sōkyū's son, Kōgetsu Sōgan, moved it to Ryūkō-in temple together with a calligraphic work by Mittan. The furnace-transmuted glaze of this bowl is not as gorgeous as that of the *Inaba Temmoku*, but many rainbow-colored crystallizations are inside of the bowl, and seven-colored luster can be seen over the dark glaze.

13
Yuteki Mottled Temmoku Type Tea Bowl.
Kaijin (Huai-ren) kiln in China. Adjunct: *Temmoku* stand with mother-of-pearl inlaid decoration of arabesque vines.

Height: 4.5cm, Mouth Diameter: 9.1cm, Foot Diameter: 3.5cm.
Southern Song dynasty, 12th–13th centuries.
Ryūkō-in temple, Kyoto.
Important Cultural Property.

This is a rather small *Temmoku* type tea bowl with a round bottom. The clay material is relatively white, and clay slip, which includes plenty of iron, covers the surface. Black glaze is put over the layer of clay slip, producing the crystallization of *Yuteki* mottled *Temmoku*. The foot of this bowl, which was carved out, is relatively large. As a whole, it is similar to the *Yuteki* mottled *Temmoku* type tea bowls from the Ken (Jian) kiln, but the method of crystallization and the tone of the glaze are entirely different. Recently, the Kaijin (Huai-ren) kiln, where the same style of *Yuteki* mottled *Temmoku* type tea bowls had been produced, was excavated in the Xiao-yu valley in Huai-ren prefecture in Shanzi province. This tea bowl was owned by the rich merchant Tennōji-ya Tsuda Sōkyū, and later, when his son Kōgetsu Sōgan entered into the priesthood, he took it with him to Ryūkō-in temple for daily use. This bowl is accompanied by a black lacquered *Temmoku* stand of foliate shape with mother-of-pearl inlaid decoration of chrysanthemum and arabesque vines. Inscriptions in gold, one arranged in the shape of the Chinese character "ten" and the other one arranged in the shape of a "Fundō"-weight, are written on the back of the stand. This bowl is an especially excellent piece among the extant *Yuteki* mottled *Temmoku* type small tea bowls of similar kind in Japan.

14
Bluish White Porcelain Sake Bottle with Engraved Design of Clouds.

One of a pair of bottles.
Mouth Diameter: 4.2cm, Height: 26.2cm,
Bottom Diameter: 9.5cm.
Southern Song dynasty, 13th century.
Danzan shrine, Nara.

This bottle has been kept in Danzan shrine in Nara as a container for *sake*-wine to be offered to deities. It is kept in a *Shunkei* lacquered box which is placed on a stand with four legs and decorative metal fittings. An old sheet of paper with the phrase "a pair of celadon vases" written on it is attached to the box. The bottle was crafted in the so-called "Mei-ping" style. A raised belt surrounds the mouth, and curling clouds are engraved around the body in the style of arabesque vines. As the clay contains plenty of iron, unglazed parts such as the foot of the bottle have turned reddish-brown. All of the bottle, with the exception of the area surrounding the foot and the inside of the foot, is coated with a relatively thick layer of dull bluish-white glaze. There are "stains" here and there on the crackled areas probably because the bottle was really used as a *Sake* bottle. This bottle is a rare object among the preserved ceramics.

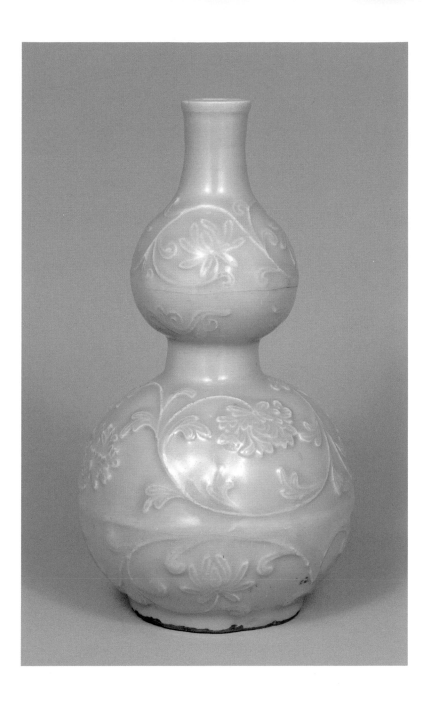

15
Celadon Bottle in the Shape of a
Gourd with Patched Decoration
of Peonies and Arabesque Vines.
Appellation: "Gankai".
Ryūsen (Long-quan) kiln in China.

Height: 27.0cm, Mouth Diameter: 3.9cm,
Bottom Diameter: 9.1cm.
Southern Song–Yuan dynasties, 13th–14th
centuries.
Manshu-in temple, Kyoto.

A gourd-shaped bottle which is called "Hu-lu Ping" in China. In Japan it was used as a flower vase. The color of the glaze is beautiful. The patched decorations are divided into four sections: Lotus flowers and vines, peonies and vines, mushrooms and clouds, and lotus flowers and vines are the subjects of the four sections from the bottom upwards. The bottle was once used as a hanging flower vase, and the mark, where the fittings used to be attached, is covered by red lacquer. The name of this vase, "Gankai" (Yan-hui), which is the name of the No. 1 disciple of Confucius, is written in black lacquer over the red lacquer. The bottle was imported to Japan before the Momoyama period and probably ever since has been preserved as a flower vase.

16-1
Vases in the Son Shape with Five-colored Decorations of Dragons, Clouds, and Flowers. Inscription: "Produced during the Wan-li era in the Ming dynasty". **Keitokuchin (Jing-de-zhen) kiln.**

Height: 59.3cm, Mouth Diameter: 21.5cm, Bottom Diameter: 18.5cm (each). Ming dynasty, 16th–17th centuries. Honnō-ji temple, Kyoto.

A pair of hexagonal large flower vases. The date of production is inscribed in cobalt-blue underneath the glazing near the rim of the mouth. The inscription in ink on the old case for these vases says: "Donation. *Nishiki-de* large flower vases. A pair. From the tea-house owner Nakajima Chōemon Shigeyoshi. October 12, in the second year of Shōhō (1645)". These two vases cannot be from the production of the governmental kiln but they are representative examples of *Manreki Akae*-type porcelains.

17
Purple Clay Water Pitcher.
Gikou (Yixing) kiln.

Height: 14.6cm, Mouth Diameter: 10.0cm,
Bottom Diameter: 9.8cm.
Ming dynasty, 16th–17th centuries.
Mampuku-ji temple, Kyoto.

Reportedly brought to Japan by the Zen monk Ingen (1592-1673). The pitcher is thought to have been made in the Yi-Xing kiln in Jian-su province, where the most excellent clay basins were produced in China in those days. As the pitcher has been in use for a long time, pear-peel-like fine mottles are on the surface. It is one of the oldest utensils for leaf-tea ceremonies that have been kept in Japan. The pitcher is notable in that its original owner is known.

◀ **16-2**
Porcelain Case (Incense Burner)
with Five-Colored Decorations
of Lotus Flowers, Vines, and
Dragons.
Inscription: "Produced during the
Wan-li era in the Ming dynasty".
Keitokuchin (Jing-de-zhen) kiln.

Height: 10.0cm, Mouth Diameter: 26.2cm,
Bottom Diameter: 22.0cm.
Ming dynasty, 16th–17th centuries.
Honnō-ji temple, Kyoto.

An oblong container with four legs. Holes were opened later in the lid for the purpose of using the container as an incense burner. It is a typical *Manreki*-type container which forms a set together with a pair of large flower vases owned by the same temple. An inscription on the lid says: "Donation. *Nishiki-de* incense burner. One item. From the tea-house owner Nakajima Chōemon Shigeyoshi. October 12, in the second year of Shōhō (1645). Honshō-in lodging section of the temple". The written seal "Nichizen" was added. The container is a valuable *Manreki*-type porcelain which came to Japan very early.

ROOM 4

Japanese ceramics are displayed in this room, showing the characteristics of the producing areas, periods, and the styles of kilns.

The earliest pieces are unglazed Sue-ki and ash-glazed earthenware. Seto pottery is the only glazed ware in a real sense in the Middle Ages (13th~16th century) and it reflects the Chinese influence clearly.

Unglazed ware of the Sue-ki type can be found in Tokoname, Atsumi, Bizen, Shigaraki, Tamba, and Echizen kilns. In them Japanese aesthetic characteristics can be seen. In the Pre-Modern Age (16th~ 19th century), because of the popularity of the tea ceremony, pottery came to be widely used. Kiseto, Setoguro, Shino-Oribe, Bizen, Karatsu, Agano, Takatori potteries produced a revolution in ceramic ware.

Porcelain manufacture started on a full scale at the end of the 16th century, and colorful styles such as early-Imari, Kakiemon, Ko-Imari, Nabeshima, and Ko-Kutani ware were made.

Kyō-yaki ware, manufactured in Kyoto is also exhibited. In the 17th and 18th centuries, Ninsei and Kenzan potteries and Ko-Kiyomizu style in Kyoto formed a main stream in this field. Later (18th~19th century), not only pottery but also porcelain was manufactured in Kyoto, reflecting the taste of each period, and Kyoto became a leader in the making of ceramics in Japan.

18
Ash-glazed Jar with Four Legs.
Sanage kiln.

Height: 16.6cm, Mouth Diameter: 9.5cm,
Bottom Diameter: 16.3cm.
Excavated from Otowa-yama, Kiyomizu-
dera temple.
Sanage kiln.
Late Heian period, 10th century.
Kiyomizu-dera temple, Kyoto.

This jar is a cinerary container for cremated ash reportedly excavated from Otowa-yama hill behind Kiyomizu-dera temple in January, 1925. Two horizontal belts are laid around the body and four legs are attached to the jar. The shape of the jar is modeled as if a wooden stand was attached to it. Ash-glaze covers the entire surface. It was produced in the Sanage kiln in Aichi prefecture, where not only ash-glazed ware but also brown-glazed and green-glazed jars with four legs were manufactured.

19
Temmoku type Seto Porcelain
Round Inkstone.
Seto kiln.

Height: 2.3cm, Mouth Diameter: 18.0cm,
Bottom Diameter: 17.3cm.
Muromachi period, 15th century.
Manshu-in temple, Kyoto.

    This inkstone made of porcelain has been kept in Manshu-in temple in Rakuhoku, Kyoto. A shallow groove is running along the rim and a half-cylindrical ink well is in the center. The area surrounding the ink well was left unglazed. Dark brown glaze is added over the line-engraved decoration of arabesque vines on the inkstone. The bottom is flat. This inkstone was made in the Seto kiln in Aichi prefecture, and it is quite rare that a piece of *Seto* ware has been preserved.

20
Iga Ware Flower Vase.
Known as "Ogura Iga".

Height: 28.3cm, Mouth Diameter: 10.6cm,
Bottom Diameter: 12.0cm.
Momoyama period, 16th century.
Important Cultural Property.

The strong intention of the artist is well reflected in the shape of this flower vase, which is one of the representative pieces of the Momoyama period. At the auction of the Akaboshi Family treasures, Mr. Tsunekichi Ogura made the successful bid and acquired this flower vase. Since then, it has been called "Ogura Iga". Two vertical lines are impressed on the front of the body, and the part between the lines is standing out. Long and slender handles are attached to both sides. Ash-glaze scattered over the entire vase produced varied decorations. The green-colored glaze showing a flow pattern on the front of the vase is especially brilliant. The bottom is flat and the lower part of the body is burnt black. There is a mark on the back of the vase where once a hole for a ring handle had been attached.

21
**Kokiyomizu Type Incense Burner
in the Shape of Lotus with
Polychrome Overglaze Painting.**
Attributed to Nonomura Ninsei.

Height: 26.4cm, Mouth Diameter: 24.2cm,
Bottom Diameter: 20.2cm.
Edo period, 17th century.
Hōkongō-in temple, Kyoto.
Important Cultural Property.

The body of this burner represents a lotus seed, its lid represents a lotus leaf, and its foot represents a lotus flower. The Sanskrit incantation of the Senju-kannon (Sahasrabhuja with thousand arms) is engraved into the lid in open-work. The motifs of the decorations are Buddhistic subjects. The foot in the shape of a lotus flower is decorated with *Rimpō* Buddhist ritual rings and arabesque vines, and the lid-knob is decorated with a *Kongōsho* Buddhist ritual pestle and lotus seed. Mainly green glaze similar to that of the Kōchi (Cohin) ware was used, and reddish-purple glaze was added. Gold was used for decoration. The old inscription on the case says: "Large lotus incense burner, made by Ninsei". An inscription on the bottom says: "Because of damage, made on July 28 in the Tempo era". This incense burner is attributed to Ninsei, but it does not bear his seal. It is a typical *Kokiyomizu* type ware with a polychrome overglaze painting, representative of the early *Kyō-yaki* pottery.

22
Tea Bowl with Sabi'e Lacquered Decoration of Narcissi.
Bearing the seal of Ninsei.

Height: 8.6cm, Mouth Diameter: 12.4cm,
Foot Diameter: 4.0cm.
Edo period, 17th century.
Tennei-ji temple, Kyoto.

This tea bowl belongs to the complete set of tea ceremony tools which Kanamori Sōwa (1584-1656) donated to Tennei-ji temple, to which both he and his mother belonged as parishioners. The characteristics of the Ninsei kiln can be recognized in the shape of the bowl. There is a layer of white clay under the glaze on which narcissi are depicted in low relief, with *Sabi'e* lacquer added. *Sabi'e* lacquer is used around the flowers in the manner of *Fukizumi* spray decoration. This bowl is a typical work which reflects Sōwa's taste. The small seal of "Ninsei" is impressed into the foot of this bowl.

23
Gosu-Akae-utsushi Type
Porcelain Dish with Decoration
of Four Deities and Twelve
Horary Animals.
By Okuda Eisen.

Height: 2.8cm, Mouth Diameter: 17.6cm,
Bottom Diameter: 9.0cm.
Edo period, 18th century.
Daitō-in temple, Kyoto.
Important Art Object.

This dish was made by using the *Gosu-Akae-utsushi* technique. That technique was invented by Eisen (1753–1811), who adopted porcelain manufacturing techniques for producing *Kyō-yaki* ware. The decoration of this dish is modeled after decorations found on Chinese bronze mirrors. Twelve horary animals are depicted in a circle, and within the circle four deities are depicted in a smaller circle. The knob in the center is round. This dish is a notable example which reflects both the Chinese influence and the taste of Japanese literati of those days. On the bottom, the *Kaō* style autograph "Eisen" is written in red.

ROOM 5·6·7

In the Heian period (9th～12th century) mainly wood was used for sculpture. The earlier items were made out of one solid wood piece, but since the 11th century, jointed wooden sculptures have become popular. The surface was lacquered and gold-foiled, or colored or left without coating.

In the early Heian period (9th century) the style of sculpture still reflected the Chinese influence, but between the end of the 10th and the early 11th centuries, when Regent Fujiwara Michinaga and Yorimichi were in power, a distinctive original Japanese style was established. The style of sculpture in the late Heian period was not based on accurate modeling but on tasteful sentiment.

Unlike the sculptures of the Heian period, those of the Kamakura period (13th～14th century) are realistic, and crystal was often inserted as eye-balls for realism. Such realism can be well observed in the sculptures in Tōdai-ji and Kōfuku-ji temples in Nara, but in Kyoto, the Heian style still continued. The tradition of the Heian period when Japanese originality was formed had a lasting influence in Kyoto. In this room many of the sculptures are from Kyoto.

24
Seated Statue of Yakushi-nyorai
(Bhaiṣajyaguru-tathāgata).

Dry-lacquer with wooden core, and coated
with lacquer.
Height: 68.3cm.
Nara period, 8th century.
Jingo-ji temple, Kyoto.
Important Cultural Property.

Hair and white curl on the forehead are missing. The left hand is pointing downwards,
showing the palm, and the finger-tips rest on the left knee. the right arm is bent in such a
way that the palm of the hand faces forwards, and all the fingers are straight (known as the
hand-pose "Semui-in"). This is a classic style Yakushi-nyorai (Bhaiṣajyaguru-tathāgata) as
it does not hold a medicine case, but the original form of this statue cannot be confirmed
because both of the hands were repaired later. This figure, which is wearing a loose drapery,
is seated in a cross-legged pose with the left leg outside. The core of the body is formed
by several wood pieces jointed together and coated thickly with dry-lacquer. In general,
the statue's basic style follows the Chinese Tang style, but the Yakushi-nyorai's eyes are
wide open as if he was staring at somebody. The flow of his clothes' drapes are complicate.
There is no old document of Jingo-ji temple recording this statue and it is possible that it
was related to Takaosan-ji temple, which was the family temple of the Wake clan.

25
*Statue of Tamon-ten
(Vaiśravaṇa).*

Color on wood.
Height: 167.0cm.
Late Heian period, 11th century.
Jōruri-ji temple, Kyoto.
National Treasure.

This statue has been kept in Kyūtai Amida-dō Hall in Jōruri-ji temple together with three other guardians as a set of four guardian deities. As all of them are slightly too big for the hall's size, it is assumed that they originally belonged to some other hall. Clothes and armor are decorated gorgeously with colors and cut-gold leaf, but the designs were rare in Kyoto during that period. Furthermore, the depiction of the motif is large, which was not common in those days, either. The three other guardians, Jikoku (Dhṛtarāṣṭra), Zōjō (Virūḍhaka), and Kōmoku (Virūpākṣa) are twisting their bodies and their clothes are waving, whereas this Tamon-ten (Vaiśravaṇa) is standing upright. There are some more differences between the three guardians and Tamon-ten in respect of technique, style, and decorations. Therefore, it seems that the Tamon-ten statue was made during the late 11th century whereas the three other statues were made during the 12th century.

Kongō-Kai (Vajradhatu)

Taizō-Kai (Garbha-dhatu)

26
Wood-carved Ryōgai Mandalas.

Plain wood, partly painted.
Two plates.
Height: 45.0cm, Width: 37.7cm (each).
Late Heian period, 12th century.
Jizō-in temple, Kyoto.
Important Cultural Property.

Kongō-kai (Vajradhātu) and Taizō-kai (Garbhadhātu) Mandalas are carved on the wooden container and the lid. Both of them are made of sandalwood, and the Buddhist figures are carved in relief. The Taizō-kai Mandala is illustrated in accordance with the regular Mandala style, but the Kongō-kai Mandala is in the form of a Mandala which solely depicts the Eighty-one Saints. This is only one section — the Jōshin-e section — of a total number of nine sections of the complete Kongō-kai Mandala. Eight Myō'ō (Vidyārāja) are added at the bottom of the scene. Each Buddhist figure is carved on plain wood, and hair, eyes, and mouth are colored. In some parts of the background light colors and cut-gold leaf are used. The reverse side is lacquered in black. Although the figures are small, they are carved well in relief. The container has been kept in Konjiki-in temple at Uji Shirakawa which was established by Lady Shijō-no-Miya Hiroko.

27
Standing Statue of Bishamon-ten (Vaiśravaṇa).

Color on Wood.
Height: 135.6cm.
Late Heian period, 12th century.
Hōshō-in temple, Kyoto.
Important Cultural Property.

Hōshō-in temple was originally called Bishamon-dō Bettō-ji temple and was located within the compound of Rengeō-in temple in the south of Hōkō-ji temple, but in 1869 it was moved to today's location at Higashiyama-Gojō. This Buddhist statue was reportedly in the private possession of Ex-Emperor Go-Shirakawa. The figure represents a slender and smart-looking general, reflecting the sophisticated sense of those days. Following the style of Chinese Buddhist statues in the Song dynasty, the pupils of the eyes are made of a different wooden material and are inserted, but otherwise no influence of the Chinese style is observable. It may have been made while Ex-Emperor Go-Shirakawa was having Rengeō-in temple constructed.

29
Ankoku-dōji, one of Statue of
King Emma and Attendants.

Color on wood.
Height: 110.5cm
Kamakura period, 13th century.
Hōshaku-ji temple, Kyoto.
Important Cultural Property.

These statues had been kept in the Emma-dō Hall in front of the Nishi-Kannon-ji temple on the south-western slope of Mt. Tennō-zan until 1872. Because of the anti-Buddhist movement in the Meiji period, the Nishi-Kannon-ji temple was destroyed and the statues were moved to the near-by Hōshaku-ji temple. Shiroku, Shimei, Ankoku-dōji and Gushō-shin are arranged around Emma-ten (Yama). According to some documents including the Emma-ten Mandala, these five figures form a group. As the names of the attendants are sometimes confused, their proper names are given at the end of this article. Although these statues were made in a realistic style, they convey the threatening impression of a judge and officials of the Hell. They are excellent sculptures of the early Kamakura period.

King Emma
("Yama")

Shiroku   Shimei
("Godō Tenrin-ō")   ("Taizanfukun")
Gushō-shin   Ankoku-dōji
("Shiroku")   ("Shimei")

28
Lions.

Lacquer on wood, and painted.
Height: 47.3cm ("A" type lion), 46.7cm ("Un" type lion).
Kamakura period, 13th century.
Taihō shrine, Shiga.
Important Cultural Property.

At the end of the 12th century, the Japanese *Wayō* style was abandoned and lion dogs of an entirely new style were produced. This is a pair of lions of the "A" and "Un" types. Neither of them bears a horn on its head, which had been one of the characteristics of the lion style in the Nara period. In the Kamakura period, it is rare to find that style. The "A"-type lion is turning its ears downwards, and the "Un"-type, in contrast, is raising them. Both of them are facing the place where the worshippers are likely to stand, and each of them has the fore-leg, which is closer to the worshippers, drawn back while the other fore-leg is put forward. The heads are small. The upper parts of the bodies are big and the lower halves and legs are slender, which makes the dogs look nimble. The lions are threatening by shaking the thick strands of their manes, and this fierceness is expressed in concentrated form on their faces. These agile lions' expressions are based on the Chinese style.

30
Standing Statue of Zemmyō-shin.

Color on wood.
Height: 31.4cm.
Kamakura period, 13th century.
Kōsan-ji temple, Kyoto.
Important Cultural Property.

According to the biographies of high priests in China, a young woman, Zemmyō by name was coquetting with Priest Gishō form Silla in Korea, who was studying in China during the Tang dynasty. As he remained unruffled, Zemmyō was impressed, and since then she began to protect Priest Gishō and the code of Buddhism by transforming herself into a dragon at some time and at some other time into a huge rock. In the illustrated narrative scroll "Kegon-engi", which reportedly was edited by Priest Myō'e in Japan, Zemmyō is described more humanly. According to that scroll, she fell in love with Priest Gishō. When she saw his ship leave for his home-country, she bursted into tears like a little girl. Eventually, she overcame her deep sorrows, was spiritually awakened and jumped into the sea, wishing to protect his ship. This statue makes us think about the scene in which Zemmyō was seeing off Priest Gishō. She is no longer in deep sorrow but is staring decisively ahead of herself, making up her mind to protect the code of Kegon Buddhism. The statue is the figure of a dauntless goddess who experienced the agony of love and lust, and overcame it. Priest Gyōkan Hōin placed this statue in Kōsan-ji temple as one of the temple's three guardian deities together with Byakkō and Kasuga. Buddhist sculptor Tankei is thought to have made it.

31
Holy Deer.

Color on wood.
Height: 51.3cm (Male), 46.4cm (Female).
Kamakura period, 13th century.
Kōsan-ji temple, Kyoto.
Important Cultural Property.

The male deer is crouching with his four legs bent. The female is stretching her neck and raising her ears. The female deer stretches her fore-legs in a pose of belling. The male deer has a nimble body and is staring at the distance; one can see his high-spirited character. The female deer has a slightly round belly, and the lines of her body are lovely. These depictions reflect the sculptor's accurate observation of nature. It is assumed that the motif for these statues was borrowed from the legend of Priest Myō'e at Kasuga Shrine. The legend alleges that when Priest Myō'e visited Kasuga Shrine, thirty deer bent their knees and bowed to him near the Chū-mon Gate of Tōdai-i temple. According to the Ninna-ji temple's version of the record, "Togano-o Daimyō-jin Gokaichō-ki", this pair of deer are the holy deer which were originally placed in front of the shrine of the deities Kasuga- and Sumiyoshi-Myōjin within the compound of Sekisui-in in Kōsan-ji temple. That is the location of the small room behind the Haiden Hall in today's Sekisui-in temple. It is most appropriate that Priest Myō'e suggested to place deer at the location that is usually occupied by lion-dogs, referring to his personal experience with deer. Therefore, the date of production may have been some time during his days. Some scholars suggest the possibility that these deer were made by the sculptor Tankei.

32
Seated Statue of
Nyoirin Kannon
(Cintāmaṇi-cakra
Avalokiteśvara).

Lacquer on wood.
Height: 99.5cm.
Kamakura period, dated 1256.
Tōgen-ji temple, Kyoto.
Important Cultural Property.

Eight scrolls of the *Hokekyō* sutra, nineteen scrolls of other Buddhist texts, and sutra cases were kept within this statue. According to the postscript of one of these Buddhist texts, Priest Enkū became the initiator for making these duplicates in Hachijō-in Dai Jion-ji temple in 1256. It is assumed that Priest Enkū is identical with Priest Risshin VI of Nishiyama Sankō-ji temple. Most likely, Priest Enkū has not only been engaged in duplicating these sutras but also in the creation of this sculpture — he probably ordered it. The Chinese influence of the Song dynasty is clearly observable on the face and hair and in the expression of drapery. These characteristics resemble the style of sculptor Jōkei (who was Bettō in Higo), but in comparison with Jōkei's statue of Shō Kannon (Avalokiteśvara) in Kurama-dera temple, this statue belongs to a group of statues made in a more formal style.

ROOM 8

Buddhist painting is one of the most important categories in Japanese painting in the Ancient and Middle Ages. Buddhist paintings consist of figure paintings both for worship services and ritual use, illustrations for Buddhist legends, and decorations for temples.

In regard to the motifs, there are three groups, according to the three schools of Buddhism: Orthodox, Esoteric, and Jōdo Buddhism. Orthodox Buddhism started in the Nara period. It covers several Buddhist sects, and worships Buddha, Bhaiṣajyaguru (Yakushi-nyorai), and Maitreya (Miroku-bosatsu). Esoteric Buddhism started in the Heian period, when priest Kūkai brought it back from Tang China. It worships Mahāvairocana (Dainichi-nyorai) as a central figure. Geometrical Mandala paintings and the angry figure of Acalanātha (Fudō-myō'ō) belong to this Buddhism. Amitābha (Amida-nyorai) and His Heaven in the west are the central idea in Jōdo Buddhism, and scenes of Amitābha descending and Heaven in the west were often painted.

The basic technical steps of Buddhist paintings were sketching, coloring, and contour-lining. Various decorative designs and patterns were added in order to express the virtue of the figures. Buddhist paintings in the Heian period are especially elegant, reflecting the elaborate and sophisticated taste of the aristocrats.

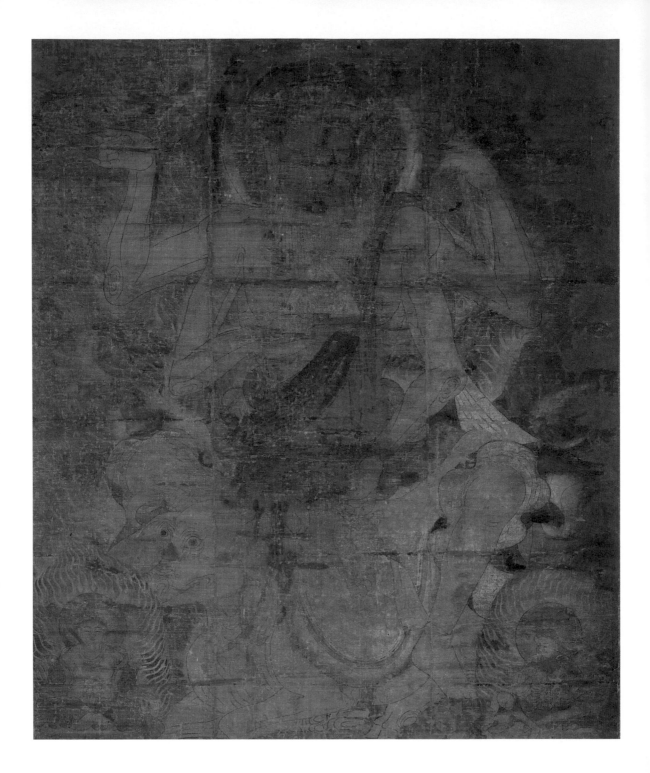

33
Ka-ten (Fire Deity).
Hanging scroll, one from a set of twelve scrolls of twelve deities or Jūni-ten.

Color on silk.
158.5 × 133.5cm.
Early Heian period, 9th century.
Saidai-ji temple, Nara.
National Treasure.

Jūni-ten are twelve deities of twelve directions who serve as guardians of the seminaries of Esoteric Buddhism. The set of paintings of the twelve deities in Saidai-ji temple is the oldest extant example, and the icons are quite similar to those in "Jutten Gyō-zō" (Icons of the twelve deities) brought from China by Priest Kūkai. Figures are depicted voluminously, and the animals, on which the deities are seated, look powerful. Judging from the continuous and smooth brush strokes and the colorings in red and green (all of which indicate the classic style), this set of paintings may have been produced during the 9th century. Among the twelve figures, the Fire Deity is notable for its careful facial expressions of an old man and the lively expression of the animal. Only a few colors and lines were added later for the purpose of repair.

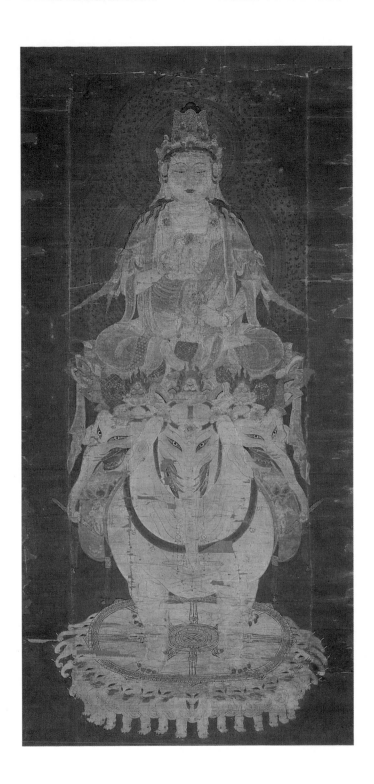

34
Fugen-Emmei.

Hanging scroll.
Color on silk.
139.0 × 66.8cm.
Late Heian period, 12th century.
Matsuo-dera temple, Kyoto.
National Treasure.

Fugen Emmei is the principal Buddhist image in the Emmei-hō Method of averting disasters and prolonging life. Especially in Enryaku-ji temple on Mt. Hiei, this method was emphasized as one of the "Four Major Rituals". It is a colorful painting, featuring neutral tints, highlighted parts in white, and white outlines. Cut-gold decorations on Fugen's drapery and cut-silver foils on the halo produce the decorative effect of this painting. Even three-headed white elephants with six tusks look natural in this painting, probably because of the expressive capability of the artist. This image is an excellent masterpiece which represents the aesthetics of Buddhist paintings in the 12th century.

35
Fudōmyō'ō (Yellow Acalanātha).

Hanging scroll.
Color on silk.
168.2 × 80.3cm.
Late Heian period, 12th century.
Manshu-in temple, Kyoto.
National Treasure.

According to the Biography of the Chief Abbot Enchin in Enryaku-ji temple of the Tendai Buddhist Sect (edited by Miyoshi Kiyoyuki), Enchin saw a golden person in the mountains during ascetic practices at the age of twenty-five. The golden figure told him that he was Fudōmyō'ō, the guardian of Enchin. Enchin immediately ordered an artist to make a sketch of him. An icon of Fudōmyō'ō in the painting style of the 9th century has been kept in Onjō-ji temple, and according to the temple, that is the very piece Enchin had ordered to sketch. The hanging scroll from Manshu-in temple shown here is a copy of the Onjō-ji version. The proportions of this figure's body are those of an adult, while the figure in the original version in Onjō-ji temple shows the proportions of a child's body. The additionally depicted rock seat in the Manshu-in version weakens the mysterious atmosphere, but this scroll is the oldest extant copy of the Yellow Acalanātha, and its elegant touch makes this painting so atrractive.

48

36
Shaka-nyorai
(Śākya Tathāgata).

Hanging scroll.
Color on silk.
159.4 × 85.5cm.
Late Heian period, 12th century.
Jingo-ji temple, Kyoto.
National Treasure.

The number of Shaka (Śākyamuni or Buddha) paintings and sculptures produced during the Heian period appears to have decreased because of the popularity of Esoteric Buddhism and Jōdo Buddhism. However, the actual number of paintings and sculptures of Shaka were as many as in the previous period as faith in Shaka existed throughout the period and was supported by the circulation of the *Hokekyō* sutra. This scroll is the only extant Buddhist painting made in the Heian period which depicts solely Shaka seated cross-legged on the seven-fold lotus seat. This painting has been called "Aka Shaka" (Red Shaka) because of the color of Shaka's drapery. His body is yellowish-white and is outlined in red flowing strokes. His drapery is decorated with *Shippō-tsunagi* patterns in cut-gold leaves, and highlighted parts are colored white. An elegant face and mild colorings produce the graceful atmosphere of this painting. It can be regarded as the most excellent icon of Tathāgata among Heian-period Buddhist paintings.

37
Star Mandala.

Hanging scroll.
Color on silk.
165.0 × 133.0cm.
Late Heian period, 12th century.
Kumeta-dera temple, Osaka.
Important Cultural Property.

The idea of correlation between planetary phenomena and human affairs was familiar to ancient people. This Star Mandala can be considered as an interpretation of that idea from the Esoteric Buddhist point of view. It is also called "Hokuto (Polar Star) Mandala" and has been used as a principal object of worship in the "Hokuto-hō" Method, which is a typical astrological method of Esoteric Buddhism praying for the prevention of disasters and the prolonging of life. There are two types of Star Mandala paintings: square-based and circle-based. This Mandala is a representative example of the square-type. Ichiji-Chōrinnō (Ekakṣara-uṣṇīṣa-cakra) is the principal figure, surrounded by the seven stars of the Great Bear, nine planets, twelve signs and the twenty-eight signs of the zodiac as deities. The descriptions of these deities are characterized by the free brush strokes in the icon style and clear colorings. This Mandala is a painting of the 12th century which was indicative of the coming new style of Buddhist paintings of the Kamakura period.

38
Fugen (Samantabhadra) and
Ten Rasetsunyo (Raksasi).

Hanging scroll.
Color on silk.
97.5 × 66.9cm.
Late Heian period, 12th century.
Rozan-ji temple, Kyoto.
Important Cultural Property.

The *Hokekyō* sutra, which was very popular and feverishly worshipped during the Heian period, introduced many Buddhist guardian deities. Fugen-bosatsu (Samantabhadra) was one of them and has become the principal image of a ritual in the Tendai sect, and the figure was painted repeatedly for general worship services. In the "Darani-bon" chapter of the *Hokekyō* sutra, Yakuō-bosatsu (Bhaiṣajya-rāja-bodhisattva), Yuse-bosatsu, two Devas, and ten Rasetsunyo (Raksasi) are introduced as the guardians of those who believe in Hokke Buddhism. This painting depicts those guardians. Fugen-bosatsu is seated on elephant-back and the ten Rasetsunyo and Kishibojin (Hariti) in Chinese cloths are standing around him well-orderly. The motions of the figures are hardly described and the painting style, using silver and gold, creates a feminine and calm atmosphere.

39
Butsugen-Butsumo
(Buddha-locana).

Hanging scroll.
Color on silk.
193.1 × 128.8cm.
Kamakura period, 12th century.
Kōsan-ji temple, Kyoto.
National Treasure.

Buddha's Eye, which is able to recognize all phenomena, is personified as Butsugen-Butsumo (Buddha-locana) in Esoteric Buddhism. Butsugen-Butsumo is wearing a lion-shaped crown, but otherwise the image is similar to Chūson Dainichi-nyorai (Mahavairocana-tathāgata) of the Taizōkai (Garbhadhātu) Mandala. This icon was in the possession of the high priest Myō'e of Kōsan-ji temple in the early Kamakura period, and Priest Myō'e reportedly cut off his ears in front of this icon. This painting represents several aspects of the new Buddhist painting style, such as a slender body viewed from a high point, the smart look with slanting eyes, the decoration of the drapery with gold clay pigment instead of cut gold leaf, and fresh colorings with white as the major color. The inscription by the figure was composed and written by Priest Myō'e. It is a rare inscription which expresses the personal relationship between the possessor and the icon.

40
Hokekyō Mandala.

Hanging scroll.
Color on silk.
144.0 × 132.0cm.
Kamakura period, 12th–13th centuries.
Kaijusen-ji temple, Kyoto.
Important Cultural Property.

This is the visual rendition of the *Hokekyō* sutra in the style of a Mandala which illustrates the general idea of the *Hokekyō* sutra through the selection of some major chapters such as "Jō-bon", "Kenhōtō-bon", "Myōon-bon" and "Jūji-yujutsu-bon". The main scene is "Shaka's sermon on Mt. Ryōju-sen" based on the chapter "Jō-bon" at the top-right of the painting. Byakugō-light emanates from the white curl between Shaka's eye-brows while he is preaching to his audience. The light illuminates all the realms from Heaven to Hell. Although it is a large-scale painting, fine depictions are shown, which indicates the influence of the popular decorative fly-leaf paintings of the *Hokekyō* sutra scrolls of those days. Mild colorings reflect the Buddhist painting style of the Heian period, but the composition of the painting, viewed from a high point, suggests that it was produced during the Kamakura period.

41
Office of the Judge in Hell.
"Effect of Prayers" in the *Hiyu-kyō*
Sutra
Hanging scroll, one from a set of
fifteen.

Color on silk.
155.5 × 68.0 cm.
Kamakura period, 13th century.
Shōjūraigō-ji temple, Shiga.
National Treasure.

The Buddhist text *Ōjō Yōshū* by Priest
Eshin Sōzu, a leading figure of the Tendai
sect of Jōdo Buddhism, introduced six
abominable realms (Heaven, Human, Ashura,
Beasthood, Starvation, Hell), and stated
that by offering prayers one can be salvated
from those six realms. This painting illustrates
the idea of that text. According to the inscription on the shaft, the scroll was owned by
Yokawa Reizan-in temple on Mt. Hiei. A weird
realm, which looks quiet but is filled with
despair, and the realm of torture in Hell,
both depicted in dark tones, are the masterpieces among the paintings of the Six Realms.
Some of the scrolls in this set of fiteen scrolls
were painted in a lively style like the paintings of the Song dynasty in China, while
others were painted in a mild *Yamato-e style*.
These two scrolls belong to the former style.
The additional scene of breaking the door of
Hell described at the bottom of the "Effect of
Prayers" belongs to the scenes of salvation
which became popular through the influence
of the paintings of the Six Realms in the
Kamakura period.

42
Descent of Amida (Amitābha)
and Twenty-five Attendants
from Heaven.
Known as "Rapid Descent".

Hanging scroll.
Color on silk.
145.1 × 154.5 cm.
Kamakura period, 13th–14th centuries.
Chion-in temple, Kyoto.
National Treasure.

Amida (Amitābha) and twenty-five attendants are descending from Heaven on clouds above a steep mountain in order to accompany a dead person, who is depicted at the bottom-right corner, on his journey to Heaven. This scene is known as "Rapid-Descent". The depiction of flying clouds, expressing speedy descent, and the description of the figures by using gold for bodies and cloths are the characteristics of Buddhist paintings in the late Kamakura period. This is a scene of "Jō-bon Jōshō-zu", which illustrates the highest state of death, because the dead person is seated upright in front of a sutra scroll and a pagoda is in the air at the top-right of the scene. The mountains in the background are rising, but the contour lines are smooth, which produces the *Yamato-e*-like gentle atmosphere. Although it is an imaginary landscape, its expression is impressive.

43
Screen of Heaven and Hell.

A pair of trwo-fold screens.
Color on silk.
101.0 × 84.0cm (each).
Kamakura period, 14th century.
Konkai-kōmyō-ji temple, Kyoto.
Important Cultural Property.

    This painting has an uncommon composition: The ocean spreads horizontally in the center of the scene, this world is depicted in front of the ocean, and the Jōdo Paradise is behind the ocean. This screen belongs to a pair of standing screens, and its counterpart represents Amida (Amitābha) appearing from the other side of the mountain with five-colored threads attached to his finger. This pair of screens seems to have been used at the death-bed. Life and death of good and bad people are described in the section of "this world". In the section of the "Jōdo Paradise", bad people are punished, and next to this scene is a scene of salvation through prayers. This painting illustrates the idea that only through the mercy of Amida and prayers to him can one escape from the abominable land. The notable point of this painting is the appearance of Jizō (Kṣitigabha). The seated figure of a transformed Jizō is confronting the Judge of Hell, and another Jizō is depicted in the scene of the Jōdo Paradise. It can be said that this new composition style of including Jizō reflects the popularity of the faith in Jizō in the Kamakura period. The painting was done in a lively miniature style. It is an outstanding masterpiece among the Jōdo Buddhist paintings of the late Kamakura period.

ROOM 9

In this room mainly ink painting and Zen painting – ink paintings of Buddhist figures and portraits of priests – are exhibited.

When Zen Buddhism was introduced from China in the late 14th century, Zen art which was different from previous Buddhist art became popular in Kyoto and Kamakura. Among several styles of Zen art, ink paintings attracted people by their simple but strong expression with ink: the "color" of ink (intensity or quality) indicated various hues and the brush strokes seemed to express the idea of Zen Buddhism itself.

Until the end of the 14th century, simple portraits of priests and other human figures were mainly painted, but in the 15th century landscape paintings with poetry became popular, led by Josetsu and Shūbun. The painting style also came to be influenced by the court paintings of the Southern Song in China. In the late 15th century the master artist Sesshū developed his own aesthetic qualities in ink paintings to create an independent area in the fine arts. In the 16th century, Kanō Motonobu and Sō'ami started to depict seasonal scenes on screens and doors as interior decoration, and this decorative feature of painting was handed down to the following Momoyama period.

In order to appreciate ink paintings, we must first locate ourselves in the painting.

Every January, this room is used for the special exhibition of the works by Tomioka Tessai, a modern literati artist in Kyoto.

Daruma (Bodhidharma)

44
Daruma (Bodhidharma), Gama
(Toad), Tekkai (Te-guai).
By Minchō.

Three hanging scrolls.
Color on paper.
241.0 × 147.5cm (Daruma), 230.0 ×
118.0cm (Gama, Tekkai).
Muromachi period, 15th century.
Tōfuku-ji temple, Kyoto.
Important Cultural Property.

There are many extant works of Minchō, the priest-artist (1352-1431) in Tōfuku-ji temple. Among them, this set of scrolls as well as "Five Hundred Arhats" and "Nirvana" (both of which are kept in Tōfuku-ji temple) are large-scale masterpieces. The central scroll represents the seated Daruma (Bodhidharma) in a cave. The majestic appearance and the strong will of the first Zen-Buddhist patriarch are portrayed well by Minchō's strong brush strokes. On both sides of the Daruma scroll are scrolls of the wizards Gama (Toad) and Tekkai (Tie-guai), which is an interesting arrangement. The postures of these two figures were obviously borrowed from the painting of "Gama and Tekkai" (kept in Chion-ji temple) by the Chinese painter Yan Hui. In comparison with the original composition by Yan Hui, pine trees and distant mountains were added to these scrolls. This interesting set of scrolls indicates how Japanese artists adopted Chinese styles.

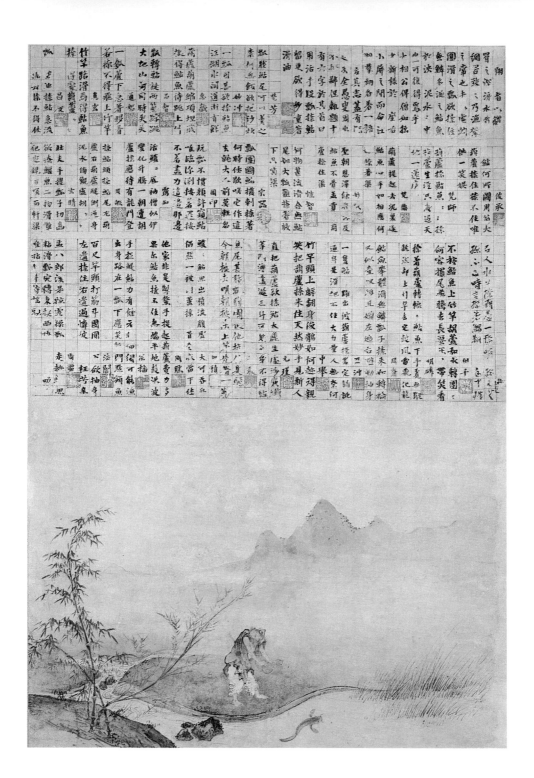

45
Hyōnen-zu (Catfish and Gourd).
By Josetsu.

Hanging scroll.
Ink and light color on paper.
111.5 × 75.8cm.
Muromachi period, 15th century.
Taizō-in temple, Kyoto.
National Treasure.

This scroll illustrates a question of Zen Buddhism: "How is it possible to catch an eely catfish with a round and slippery bottle-gourd?". The inscriptions in poetry-style above the painting are answers to this question given by Priest Daigaku Shūsū and thirty-one monks. Priest Daigaku Shūsū was the representative of the five major temples in those days. According to the foreword by Priest Shūsū, Shogun Ashikaga Yoshimochi suggested to make this painting, and Priest Josetsu painted it. This hanging scroll originally was a standing screen with the painting on one side and the inscriptions on the other side. This painting is meaningful as one of the earliest works by the artist, who was actively studying Chinese Court painting styles such as Ma Yuan's, Liang Kai's etc. It seems that this painting even set the direction of the ink paintings of the Muromachi period.

46
Screen of Bamboo, Rocks and Cranes.
Attributed to Kanō Masanobu.

Six-fold screen.
Ink on paper.
156.5 × 356.0 cm.
Muromachi period, 15th century.
Shinju-an temple, Kyoto.
Important Cultural Property.

Although this screen does not bear a seal, it was reportedly painted by Kanō Masanobu (1434-1530), the founder of the Kano school. This screen possibly was the left-hand piece of a pair of screens, since most of the subjects are shown on the left side, while a wide margin was left on the right. Cranes are depicted in the center, and trees and rocks are arranged around these birds. It is amazing that the delicate brush strokes even describe moist air and mild sunlight. Whether painted by Masanobu or not, this screen, as the only extant large-scale flower-and-bird painting by some painter of the early Kano school before the establishment of Kanō Motonobu's style, is a significant masterpiece.

47
Priest Hui Kuo Showing His
Amputated Arm.
By Sesshū.

Hanging scroll.
Ink and light color on paper.
199.9 × 113.6 cm.
Muromachi period, dated 1496.
Sainen-ji temple, Aichi.
Important Cultural Property.

When Bodhidharma, the patriarch of Zen Buddhism, was meditating while facing the rock wall in Shōrin-ji temple, Priest Hui Kuo came and asked Bodhidharma to be accepted as a disciple. When Bodhidharma rejected him, Hui Kuo chopped off his left arm to prove his firm determination, whereupon he was accepted. This is a famous scene of Zen Buddhism. The realistic description of faces and sharp eyes and the static composition create a strained atmosphere. This scene may represent the spiritual state at which the seventy-seven year-old Zen monk-artisu Sesshū had arrived. According to the inscription on the back, this scroll was donated to Sainen-ji temple by Saji Tamasada, the feudal lord of Miya-yama castle in Chita county in the province of Owari (today's Aichi prefecture) in 1532, which was shortly after Sesshū's death.

48
Landscape.
By Sesshū.

Hanging scroll.
Ink and light color on paper.
117.5 × 35.2 cm.
Muromachi period, 16th century.
National Treasure.

This work is considered as Sesshū's last painting. Inscriptions by Priest Mokushō Shūshō of Hōju-ji temple and Priest Ryōan Keigo of Tōfuku-ji temple, written above the landscape, express the two priests' sorrow and mourning for the loss of their best friend, the painter Sesshū. The painting depicts a man of noble character and his attendant on a steep path, winding through rocky cliffs. Tall pine trees, pavillions, and an arbor are depicted ahead of them. The brush strokes are relatively weak, probably because of Sesshū's old age, but the clear representation of perspective and the sense for a stable composition are proof of Sesshū's excellent ability.

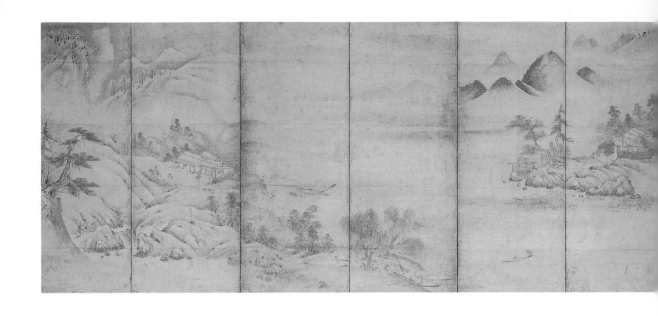

49
Screen of the Eight Scenic Views of the Xiao-Xiang Rivers.
Attributed to Sōami.

A pair of six-fold screens.
Ink on paper.
157.1 × 354.3 cm (each).
Muromachi period, 16th century.
Myōshin-ji temple, Kyoto.
Important Cultural Property.

Landscape motifs from the Eight Scenic Views of the Xiao-Xiang Rivers are described with soft and tasteful brush strokes, which the painter may have learnt by studying Mu Qi's or Gao Ranhui's paintings. Unlike the clarity of the Kano school's landscape paintings, peacefulness and a sentiment, which is unique to this painting, dominate the scene and comfort the onlooker's mind. Sōami (-1525), a monk who was a retainer of the Shogun, is considered as the artist who very likely painted this screen. However, in comparison with Sōami's standard work — the sliding door panels of the Eight Views of the Xiao-Xiang Rivers in Daisen-in temple — the usage of ink in this screen is sometimes rather careless. It is, therefore, not very natural to think that this painting was made during Sōami's days. Instead, it seems more proper to suggest that it was painted by a member of the Ami school some time during the generation that succeeded Sōami's.

50
Flower-and-Bird Painting of Four Seasons.
By Kanō Motonobu.

Hanging scroll, from a set of eight scrolls.
Color on paper.
174.5 × 139.5cm (four scrolls),
174.5 × 99.0 cm (four scrolls).
Muromachi period, 16th century.
Daisen-in temple, Kyoto.
Important Cultural Property.

This work is in the Hōjō Hall (Hall of Danna) in Daisen-in temple within the compound of Daitoku-ji temple. It is counted as one of the masterpieces by Motonobu (1476-1559). The panels of eight sliding doors form a large-scale scene, which is composed neatly with a big pine-tree as its central piece. Only flowers and birds are thickly colored, creating a very vivid color-effect. This painting includes many elements which have a direct link to the gorgeous and magnificent panel paintings of the Momoyama period. The year of Daisen-in temple's foundation, 1513, is generally regarded as the date of production, but a new interesting opinion was recently put forward from the viewpoint of pre-modern architectural history, suggesting that the panel may have been made in 1535, when the large-scale renovation of Hōjō Hall was carried out.

ROOM 10

Handscroll painting, which consists of narrations and illustrations, is one of the original Japanese art styles. The style was established in the late Heian period when literature became popular and the technique of Yamato-e painting was well developed. Many handscroll paintings were made in the Kamakura and Muromachi periods.

The earlier scrolls mainly present fiction and folk tales, but in the Kamakura period biographies of master priests, the origins and legends of temples and shrines were also depicted. Several unique techniques can be seen, such as houses without roofs to show the interiors and the expression of passing time by changing the scenes horizontally without separation between the scenes on the scrolls.

There are also scrolls of portraits and sketches.

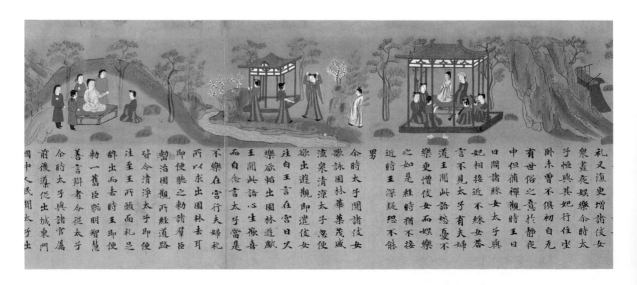

51
Illustrated Sutra of Cause and Effect.

Handscroll.
Color on paper.
26.5 × 1034.2cm.
Nara period, 8th century.
Jōbon Rendai-ji temple, Kyoto.
National Treasure.

This scroll contains the "Sutra of Cause and Effect of the Past and Presence" (four vols.), which covers the legend of the previous incarnation of Shaka (Śākyamuni) and his biography from his birth to his final enlightenment when he became Buddha. The text is written in the lower half of the scroll, and the illustrations are placed in the upper half. This scroll, which was kept in Jōbon Rendai-ji temple, is the first part of the second volume, which describes the younger days of Shaka.

This sutra is based on a copied sutra from the period of Six Dynasties in China. The painting style, which presents precise depictions in archaic simplified forms, reflects the high standard of Japanese painting in the Nara period. The method of developing the narration through successive scenes, devided by trees and rocks, and through focusing on human figures is considered as the primitive form of the illustrated narrative scrolls, which were popular in the late Heian period.

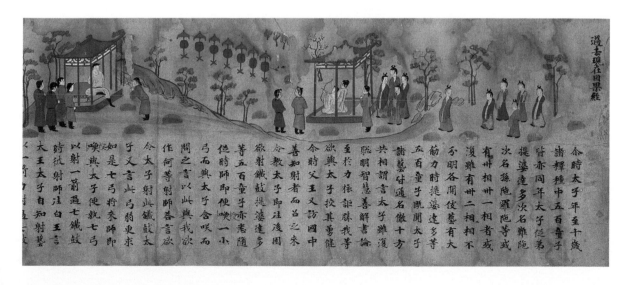

52
Legend of Kokawa-dera Temple.

Handscroll.
Color on paper.
30.8 × 1984.2cm.
Late Heian period, 12th century.
Kokawa-dera temple, Wakayama.
National Treasure.

This scroll is an illustrated legend of the central statue of Kokawa-dera temple, a sanctuary for the worship of Kannon (Avalokiteśvara). The first half (two chapters) of the scroll introduces the origin of the Hall of Senju Kannon (Sahasrabhuja or Avalokiteśvara with thousand arms), whose establishment was initiated by the petition of a hunter. The second half (three chapters) is telling the legendary story of an incarnation of Kannon who healed the sick daughter of a millionaire in Kawachi, whereupon the whole family of the millionaire thanked Kannon and entered into priesthood and worked for Kokawa-dera temple as *Bettō* monks.

The story is developed on a long scroll. A classic and simple style, such as the repeated description of the Hall of Kannon and the hunter's stool, together with the strong brush strokes of the trees and simplified mountain slopes, are apparent throughout the scroll.

53
Illustrated Biographies of the Patriarchs of Kegon Buddhism.

Handscroll from a set of six volumes.
Color on paper.
31.7 × 1219.0cm (Vol. II).
Kamakura period, 13th century.
Kōsan-ji temple, Kyoto.
National Treasure.

This is an illustrated biography of high priest Gishō (625–702) of Kegon Buddhism from Silla, Korea. The story is based on the *Biographies of High Priests in the Song Dynasty*, but the major subject is the story of Zemmyō, a woman in the Tang dynasty, who fell in love with Gishō while he was studying in China and transformed herself into a dragon for the purpose of protecting Gishō's ship when he was sailing back to Korea. The legendary nature of the story is strong. It was Priest Myō'e's intention to divinify Zemmyō as a protector of Kegon Buddhism.

Thick and strong lines and delicate lines are properly used to create dynamic scenes. These dynamic scenes are lightly and transparently colored, which suggests the influence of paintings from the Song dynasty; this kind of coloring creates the beautiful and clean atmosphere of the painting.

54
Illustrated Biography of Priest Ippen.
By Hōgen En'i.

Twelve handscrolls.
Color on Silk.
37.9 × 1020.3cm (Vol. IX).
Kamakura period, dated 1299.
Kankikō-ji temple, Kyoto: Shōjōkō-ji
temple, Kanagawa (joint ownerwhip).
National Treasure.

These scrolls are an illustrated biography which describe the life of high priest Ippen (1239–1289), who established the Jishū sect of Buddhism and spent his life popularizing prayers on his journeys. These scrolls were made by Priest Shōkai, the founder of Rokujō Dōjō (Kankikō-ji temple), in August 1299 at the tenth anniversary of Priest Ippen's death in order to thank him for his contribution. The illustrations are by Hōgen En'i.

Although the scrolls are a biography of Priest Ippen, his figure and his deeds are not overemphasized but described objectively within the depiction of the vast natural landscape. The expression of temple, shrines and landscapes is precise and was painted minutely after real scenes. Texture painting in ink, which was influenced by ink paintings of the Song and Yuan dynasties in China, is found in many areas of the scrolls, and is in extraordinary harmony with the Japanese *Yamato-e* style atmosphere.

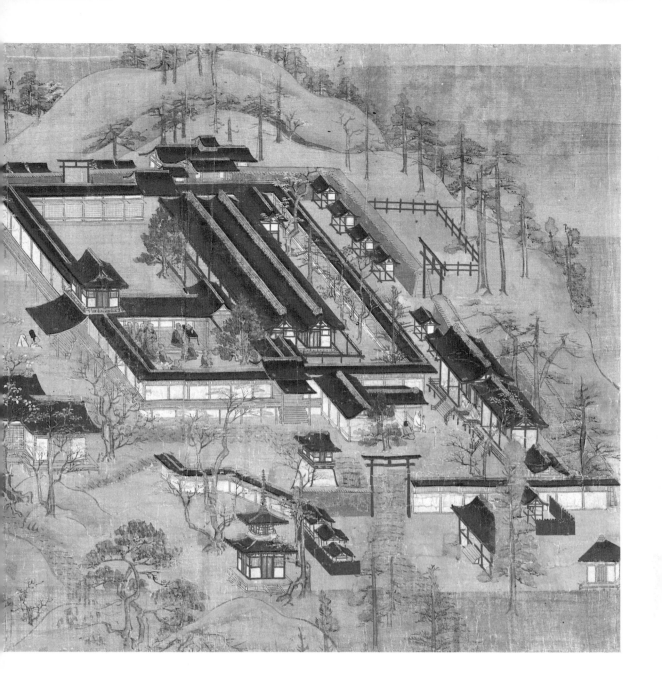

55
The Legendary Origin of
Shinnyo-dō Temple.
By Kamon-nosuke Hisakuni.

Three handscrolls.
Color on paper.
34.8 × 1921.0cm (Vol. III).
Muromachi period, dated 1529.
Shinshōgokuraku-ji temple, Kyoto.
Important Cultural Property.

These narrative scrolls contain the history of the major Buddhist statue of Shinnyo-dō temple (Shinshō Gokuraku-ji temple) in Rakutō, Shinnyo-dō temple's history, and mysterious legends pertaining to the temple. According to the postscripts of these scrolls and according to an article dated April, 1529 in the *Sanetakakō-ki* record, it is known that the narrations were written by the Emperor Go-Kashiwabara, Prince Kunitaka, Cloistered Prince Sonchin, Sanjō-nishi Sanetaka, and Ex-archbishop Kōjo. It is also known that the illustrations were painted by Kamon-nosuke Hisakuni.

This artist is not known for any other works except these scrolls. The characteristics of the *Yamato-e* style of the 16th century, such as thick and gorgeous colorings and decorative composition in gold pigment, are demonstrated well in this work. It seems Hisakuni was one of the leading artists of those days.

55

56

56
The Illustrated History of the
Origin of Kuwanomi-dera Temple.
By Tosa Mitsushige.

Two handscrolls.
Color on paper.
35.2 × 1367.3cm (Vol. I).
Muromachi period, dated 1532.
Kuwanomi-dera temple, Shiga.
Important Cultural Property.

The foundation and history of Kuwanomi-dera temple located east of Lake Biwa are illustrated in these scrolls. These scrolls were made on the petition of Shogun Ashikaga Yoshiharu, who took refuge in Ōmi (today's Shiga prefecture), and were donated to Kuwanomi-dera temple on August 17, 1532. The title and the narration of the first chapter were written by the Emperor Go-Nara and other chapters were written by the Cloistered Prince Sonchin of Seiren-in-no-miya and Sanjō-nishi Sanetaka. The illustrations were done by Tosa Mitsushige, who was Tosa Mitsuoki's son.

The shapes of the subjects and the way of expression of Mitsushige resemble his father's style, but unlike his father, he adopted the classic style in his constructive and firm composition, and his originality is evident in his depiction of the landscape of Gamouno in the bird's-eye-view. The revival of the classic style is evident in the decorative and gorgeous painting style of using thick navy-blue and greenish-blue colors on gold-foiled paper.

ROOM 8, 9,10

Portrait painting has been one of the important genres throughout the history of paintings, and various kinds of excellent portraits were painted in each period.

The Japan's history of portraits began when portraits of Buddhist patriarchs were brought to Japan. Since then, portrait-painting developed around the portraits of high priests as the major works. Those works depicted idealized human figures comparable to Buddhist paintings, and at the same time they were commemorative paintings of the high priests of the past. During the late Heian period, however, living persons, including the Emperors and court nobles, began to be portrayed, and portrait-painting in the real sense started. When Fujiwara Takanobu began to paint "Nise'e" (likeness paintings) after models, portrait-painting began to express not only the appearance of the model but also the model's personality. During the Kamakura period, when Zen Buddhism was introduced to Japan from China, portraits of Zen monks, called "Chinsō", began to be painted as certificates to be given from a master monk to his disciples when they had mastered the doctorines of Zen Buddhism. The realism of Chinese paintings of the Song dynasty influenced the depiction of human figures, and portraits became lively when a subtle three-dimentional effect was added.

In the Muromachi period portraits of military officers, such as the portrait of Shogun Ashikaga, which derived from portraits of court nobles, began to be painted. From the late Muromachi period, women and children began to be portrayed. Those paintings are important items both as paintings of human figures and as genre paintings, which emphasized costumes. During the Edo period, the portrait styles as well as the models became more varied, and portraits reflecting the originality of the leading artists were produced.

In the Kyoto National Museum portraits in the *Yamato-e* style are displayed in Room 8, portraits of Zen monks (Chinsō) are in Room 9, and the modern portraits are in Room 10. They are displayed according to their periods of production, painting styles, and models.

57
***Portrait of the Ex-Emperor
Go-Toba.***

Hanging scroll.
Color on paper.
40.6 × 30.7cm.
Kamakura period, 13th century.
Minase-jingū Shrine, Osaka.
National Treasure.

The ex-Emperor Go-Toba tried to return to political power after the death of Minamoto Sanetomo and attacked the Kamakura shogunate in 1221 (the Battle of Jōkyū). But he was defeated and was sent into exile on Oki Island, where he spent the rest of his life. It is assumed that the ex-Emperor had the master likeness-painter Fujiwara Nobuzane paint two of his portraits, in one of which he is wearing an ordinary (non-Buddhist) costume and in the other one Buddhist costume. The portrait introduced here is the one where he is wearing the ordinary costume. the special portrait technique that depicts the facial expression by many fine and light brush strokes is clearly evident, and indicate that the artist may have made a drawing in front of the ex-Emperor.

59
***Portrait of Minamoto Yoritomo
and Portrait of Taira-no-
Shigemori.***

Two hanging scrolls.
Color on silk.
143.0 × 112.8cm (Yoritomo), 143.0 ×
111.2cm (Shigemori).
Kamakura period, 13th century.
Jingo-ji temple, Kyoto.
National Treasures.

These portraits supposedly belong to the set of portraits which was kept in Sentō-in within the Jingo-ji temple compound. Other portraits in this set were those of Emperor Go-Shirakawa's, Fujiwara Mitsuyoshi's, and Taira-no-Narifusa's. Among them, these portraits of Minamoto Yoritomo and Taira-no-Shigemori's together with Mitsuyoshi's portrait are still extant.

The square shoulders of their official costumes and straight sleeves form a triangular and stable composition, which creates a grave atmosphere. These portraits reflect a new sense of art entirely different from the prevailing aestheticism during the period of the cloistered government. The design of arabesque vines on the *Hō* costume shows a freshness without formalism nor deformation. The subtle three-dimentional expression of the face indicates the spirit of realism of the early Kamakura period. This painting is attributed to Fujiwara Takanobu, who was an accomplished likeness painter. It is different from the ordinary "Nise-e" (likeness-paintings) which were usually painted on small-size paper. This work is doubtlessly a representative masterpiece of *Yamato-e* style portraits in the early Kamakura period.

高山寺栂尾山中
繩床樹定心石
拔此價生得〈く〉私
寫眞求安祥〈宝〉〈坐〉
沙〈私〉門〈髙辨〉〈碑〉

58
Portrait of Priest Myō'e.

Hanging scroll.
Color on paper.
146.0 × 58.8cm.
Kamakura period, 13th century.
Kōsan-ji temple, Kyoto.
National Treasure.

Priest Myō'e was from Kishū (today's Wakayama prefecture). He lost his parents during his childhood and entered into priesthood under his uncle, Priest Jōkaku, to study Kegon Buddhism and esoteric Buddhism. In 1206, ex-Emperor Go-Toba gave him an estate in Togano-o, and Myō'e founded a seminary there for the revival of Kegon Buddhism.

As is known from the inscription by Priest Myō'e himself, this portrait represents him sitting in meditation on a tree on Mt. Ryōga behind Kōsan-ji temple. Priest Myō'e is depicted rather small compared with the surrouding natural landscape with a forest of pine trees, which are drawn in rough brush strokes. This composition is exceptional for a portrait, but the common method of likeness painting of those days, which uses repeated fine brush strokes to describe facial expressions, can be observed, indicating that attention was paid to the likeness of Priest Myō'e.

60
Portrait of Priest Shōichi Kokushi.

Hanging scroll.
Color on silk.
165.0 × 98.0cm.
Kamakura period, dated 1279.
Manju-ji temple, Kyoto.
Important Cultural Property.

Priest Enni or Shōichi Kokushi (1202–1280) was from Suruga (today's Shizuoka prefecture). He went to China in 1235 during the Song dynasty to study under the Priest Chi-jue, Shi-tian, and Tui-geng, and he succeeded the Buddhist theory of Priest Wu-zhun Shifan in Mt. Jing-shan. Enni returned to Japan in 1241 and established the Shōten-ji and Sūfuku-ji temples in Hakata. Supported by Fujiwara Michiie and his son, Yoshizane, Enni also founded Tōfuku-ji temple in Higashiyama, Kyoto which became one of the major Zen temples in Japan.

At the beginning of his late-middle ages, he was suffering from a disease of right eye. Since then, his portraits were usually painted to show his face from the left side. The depiction is simple but impressive and represents his character to the full extent. It is one of the most outstanding portraits of Buddhist priests of the Kamakura period. The inscription at the top of the portrait was written by Enni himself. Accroding to this inscription, this portrait was given to Priest Higashiyama Tanshō, the second abbot of Tōfuku-ji temple.

61
Portrait of Miyoshi Chōkei.

Hanging scroll.
Color on silk.
107.9 × 49.9cm.
Muromachi period, dated 1566.
Jukō-in temple, Kyoto.
Important Cultural Property.

Miyoshi Chōkei, who once had been a vassal of the feudal lord Hosokawa in Awa (today's Tokushima prefecture), defeated his former lord Hosokawa Harumoto and gained power. He came to Kyoto to support the Shogun and gained influence. But later on Nagayoshi's own vassal, Matsunaga Hisahide, took Nagayoshi's place, and he died in dispair. Thus, Chōkei's life represents the social conditions of those days — the lower ranks dominating the higher ranks.

This portrait was made on the occasion of the third anniversary of Chōkei's death with an inscription written by Priest Shōrei Shūkin, who was a founder of Chōkei's family temple, Jukō-in. The figure is clad in the costume of a military officer with *Eboshi* cap and *Hitatare* formal wear. Designs of paulownia on the Hitatare and elegant stripes on the *Kosode*, showing from the collar, indicate the fashion of those days.

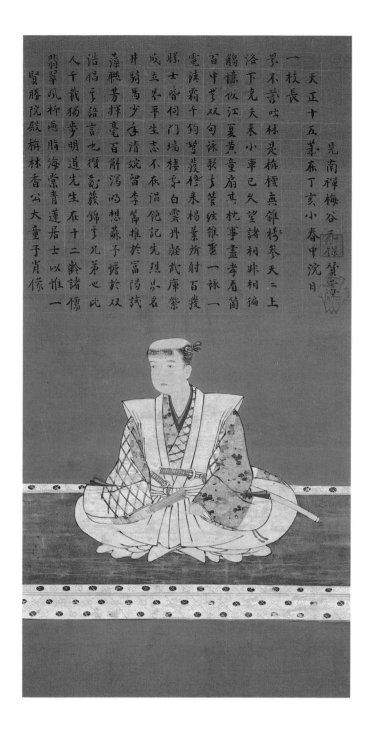

兄南禅梅谷一僕
天正十五年丙丁亥小春中浣日

賛云
一枝長

學不兼咕林灵梅檀無雜穆參天二上
洛下竞夫来小車已久望諸相非相偏
籠懐似江夏黃童扇其枕事盡孝看簡
百中芝雙句詠歌去菅紋錐篁一詠一
電漢霜千釣弩菱樨来楊葉所射百發
勝士省伺門墻棲玉白雲丹經武庫紫
成立呆平生志不在飽記先烈此其名
井騎馬少子清婉留李篤推於冨陽試
藤聰芳撰亳百解溤心想蘇子嬉於雙
結佝孝語言也償家簽遊兄第也此
人千載獨歩明道先生在十二齢諸儒
翡翠凡柳画脂海棠青蓮居士以惟一
賢勝院殿栴林香公大童子肖像

62
Portrait of Hosokawa Hasumaru.

Hanging scroll.
Color on silk.
66.7 × 33.9cm.
Momoyama period, dated 1587.
Chōshō-in temple, Kyoto.
Important Cultural Property.

Hosokawa Hasumaru (1576–87), Hosokawa Yūsai's son and Tadaoki's younger brother, died in July 1587 at the age of only twelve. His father Yūsai was lamenting his death and had his portrait painted. An inscription is written above the figure by Baiya Gempō, who was a master of Yūsai's younger brother Baiin Genchū.

The figure is clad in *Kamishimo* formal wear and is sitting on his knees in a solemn manner on the *Tatami* mat, which is rimmed in *Kōrai* (Korean) style. The *Kosode* wear, partly with a blue checkered pattern on a white background and partly chrysanthemum designs on a yellowish-green background provides important information about the *Tsujigahana* tie-dyeing method, which was popular in those days. During the Momoyama period, portraits of women and children were often made. Among them, this portrait is a representative piece of excellent quality.

ROOM 11

Screen and door panel painting in the Momoyama and Edo periods are the main exhibits in this room. When gorgeous palaces, temples and shrines were built in the Momoyama period, several pictures were painted on replaceable furniture, such as standing screens and door panels, as interior decorations. Artists of the Kanō school which had a long history from the Muromachi period, and those of the Hasegawa, Unkoku, Kaihō, and Soga schools were in charge of the paintings. In the Edo period, several other schools of artists were formed such as a literati art school, represented by Ike Taiga, and a realistic painting school by Maruyama Ōkyo.

During the Gion-matsuri festival in Kyoto, citizens exhibit their family treasure screens in their houses for visitors, and this is called the Byōbu-matsuri (screen festival).This room is similar to that festival.

63
Screens with Fan-Papers.

Two six-fold standing screens.
Color and ink on gold-foiled paper.
Muromachi–Edo periods, 15th–17th centuries.
Nanzen-ji temple, Kyoto.
Important Art Objects.

Nanzen-ji temple owns eight six-fold standing screens with decorations of fan-papers, two of which are kept in the Kyoto National Museum. As thirty fan-papers are attached to each screen, a total of two hundred and fourty fan-papers were used for all the screens. The dates of production are the mid-Muromachi and Momoyama periods, and for the latest pieces, the early Edo period. Most of the artists in charge of the production are considered to have been from the Kano school, but there are a few screens in the *Yamato-e* style. Fans used to be sent as gifts, and in Zen temples, "Katsujiki" (waiters), who served at the tables on the occasion of parties, were always carrying fans as a custom. For these reasons, so many fans were available for the production of decorative screens. Most of the fans are made of gold-foiled paper.

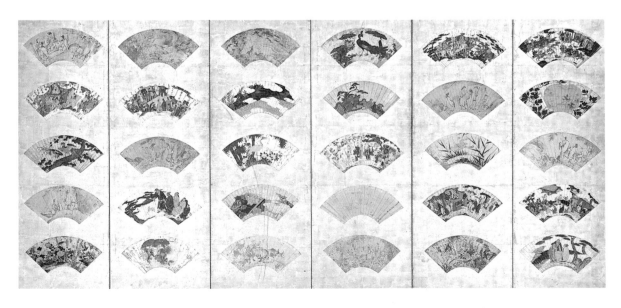

64
Screen with Fan-Papers
Illustrating Monthly Events.

Six-fold screen.
Color on gold-foiled paper.
Muromachi period, 16th century.
Kōen-ji temple, Kyoto.
Important Cultural Property.

Fan-papers illustrating the monthly events in Kyoto from January to June are attached to this screen in the style of "Floating Fan", which was an elegant game in the Court. Probably, this screen was originally accompanied by another screen with fans, which illustrated the monthly events from July to December.

A vase-shaped seal with the name "Motonobu" is stamped on each fan-paper in red, but this does not necessarily mean that Kanō Motonobu, who was the leader of the artists in the late Muromachi period, painted the illustrations on the fans. But it is at least certain that the fans were illustrated in Motonobu's studio. The scenes of Kyoto in the late Muromachi period are vividly expressed on every fan by some skillful artist. We can call it an outstanding work in the field of genre paintings of those days.

65
Waves.
Attributed to Kanō Motonobu.

Twelve hanging scrolls.
Ink on gold-foiled paper.
185.0 × 140.5cm (each).
Momoyama period, 16th century.
Zenrin-ji temple, Kyoto.
Important Cultural Property.

These hanging scrolls were originally sliding door panels. Accroding to the records in the temple, these scrolls have been attributed to Kanō Motonobu of the late Muromachi period, but the texture strokes depicting large rocks on the rough waves are obviously different from Motonobu's strokes. They rather indicate the characteristics of the Hasagawa Tōhaku's school. During the Edo period, this painting was called "Awa-no-Naruto" (The Naruto Straits in the Province of Awa). The surging waves described on these large screens fit that title, but there is probably no necessity to think of the scrolls as depicting a real-world scene. It should be appreciated that the artist aimed at representing a traditional main landscape motif in a modern manner, using gold-foiled paper and ink.

66
Old Trees and Monkeys.
By Hasagewa Tōhaku.

Two hanging scrolls.
Ink on paper.
155.0 × 115.0cm (each).
Momoyama period, 16th century.
Ryūsen-an temple, Kyoto.
Important Cultural Property.

Hasegawa Tōhaku (1539–1610) was an active artist and rivalled the Kanō school artists during the Momoyama period. The paintings are now mounted as a pair of hanging scrolls, but originally they were painted on a standing screen. This pair of paintings is taken from four panels of the original screen. Reportedly, they were formerly owned by Maeda Toshinaga, the feudal lord of Komatsu in the Province of Kaga (today's Ishikawa prefecture).

Tōhaku was from Nanao of the Noto peninsula. Hompō-ji temple was supporting him after he had moved to Kyoto. Besides, he became a favorite with Sen-no-Rikyū, a great master of tea ceremony, and he was able to visit Daitoku-ji temple frequently. This painting obviously shows the direct influence of the painting "Monkeys" by Mu Qi (National Treasure), a valuable non-Buddhistic treasure of Daitoku-ji temple brought from China.

67
Landscape.
By Unkoku Tōgan.

Four panels.
Ink on paper.
179.6 × 141.5cm (each).
Momoyama period, 16th century.
Ōbai-in temple, Kyoto.
Important Cultural Property.

These panel paintings are interior decorations in the *Hōjō* Hall (Hall of Danna) in Ōbai-in, which is one of the subordinate temples within the compound of Daitoku-ji temple. The artist is Unkoku Tōgan (1547–1618) who was serving with the feudal lord Mōri in Yamaguchi prefecture. He succeeded the ownership of Unkoku-an temple, where Buddhist priest-artist Sesshū was originally living, and entered the priesthood. This is a realistic landscape painting in Tōgan's typical style. Mountain cliffs, large rocks, and houses are well arranged with a vast range of water as the central element. It could well be one of the examples of "excellent landscape painting and well-ordered arrangement", discussed by Shirai Kayō's *Gajō Yōryaku*. Fine brush strokes and the perspective composition indicate that this is one of the earliest works among the extant paintings by Tōgan, but no record has been found that would prove its real date of production.

68
Seven Sages in the Bamboo Forest.
By Kaihō Yūshō.

Sixteen hanging scrolls.
Ink on paper.
196.5 × 185.7cm (each).
Momoyama period, 16th century.
Kennin-ji temple, Kyoto.
Important Cultural Property.

There were many sliding door panel paintings by Kaihō Yūshō (1533–1616) in the *Dai Hōjō* Hall in the *Hombō* main building in Kennin-ji temple, but when the *Dai Hōjō* Hall was damaged by the big typhoon "Muroto" in 1934 all the panel paintings were re-mounted as hanging scrolls, including the "Seven Sages in the Bamboo Forest" (16 scrolls), "Four Elegant Hobbies" (10 scrolls), "Dragons and Clouds" (8 scrolls), "Landscape" (8 scrolls), and "Flowers and Birds" (8 scrolls). It is assumed that all of them were painted around 1599 when the *Dai Hōjō* Hall was renovated. The "Seven Sagas in the Bamboo Forest" was originally painted on the sliding door panels of the eastern, northern, and western sides of the *Dai Hōjō* Hall. The brush strokes of figures and the forest are free and easy without being particular about details. Therefore, the figures of this painting are called "sack-like figures of Yūshō".

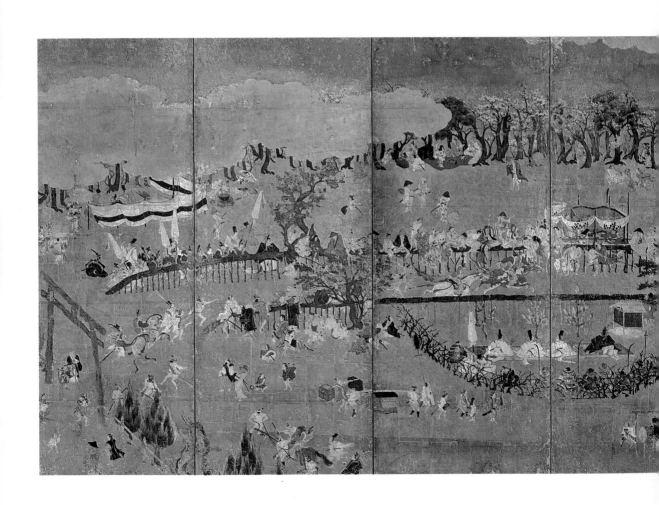

69
Screen of Dragon and Tiger.
By Kanō Sanraku.

A pair of six-fold screens.
Color on gold-foiled paper.
178.0 × 379.0cm (each).
Momoyama period, 16th century.
Myōshin-ji temple, Kyoto.
Important Cultural Property.

In Myōshin-ji temple there are tall standing screens with paintings of "Three Sages Tasting Vinegar, Han-shan, and Shi-de", "Four Elegant Hobbies", and "Flowering Plants", which are well-known as masterpieces of Kaihō Yūshō. The screen of "Dragon and Tiger", which is introduced in this article, used to be considered as Yūshō's work, too, according to the record "Shōhōsan-shi" of the Edo period, but the texture strokes of the rocks are obviously different from those of Yūshō's. It is more proper to think that Kanō Sanraku (1559–1635) painted this screen. This picture, describing the confrontation of a dragon and a tiger, gives a stronger impression than many other paintings of the same subject, probably because the artist belonged to the *Samurai* class.

A leopard is depicted at the side. In those days, people mistook leopards for female tigers.

71
Screens of the Horce Race in Kamo.

A pair of six-fold screens.
Color on paper.
153.5 × 358.0cm (each).
Edo period, 17th century.
Important Art Object.

Horce racing, held on May 5 at Kamigamo Shrine as an annual shrine event, is, just like the Gion-e festival, one of the representative festivals in Kyoto. All racing horses are named after Kamigamo Shrine's manors, and people predict the amount of harvest from each of the shrine manors by referring to the performance of the horses.

There are many works of art which illustrate the horse race in Kamo. The later works reveal the artists' interest in the speedy race itself more obviously, but the artist of this screen did not forget that the horse race was a shrine event and put equal emphasis on the depiction of the shrine compound and buildings. The human figures, represented in a unique phlegmatic expression, are outstanding in comparison with many pre-modern genre paintings.

70
Screens of the Wind God and the
Thunder God.
By Tawaraya Sōtatsu.

A pair of two-fold screens.
Color on gold-foiled paper.
169.8 × 154.5cm (each).
Edo period, 17th century.
Kennin-ji temple, Kyoto.
National Treasure.

Although these screens do not bear any inscription nor seal, nobody would have any doubt that these screens were painted by Tawaraya Sōtatsu (whose dates of birth and death are unknown). Ogata Kōrin, and later Sakai Hōitsu, copied these paintings because they, too, believed that it was painted by Sōtatsu.

Gold foils make the painted subjects stand out against the background, and at the same time they naturally achieve the decorative effect of gold. Besides, gold foils produce a space with limitless depth in these screens. Gold foils are meaningful not only as a decorative material but also as a material for representing demonic deities in the midst of the boundless space. For this reason, these screen paintings are masterpieces.

74
Screens of a Kyokusui Poetry
Party at Rantei.
By Kanō Sansetsu.

Two pairs of eight-fold screens.
Color on gold-foiled paper.
107.5 × 237.6cm (each).
Edo period, 17th century.
Zuishin-in temple, Kyoto.
Important Cultural Property.

According to the temple record, the
artist who painted these screens was Kanō
Sanraku, but judging from the painting style,
his son-in-law, Kanō Sansetsu (1590–1651)
should have been the painter. Regardless of
the extraordinarily large painting space, which
consists of two pairs of eight-fold screens,
a gorgeous and decorative atmosphere pre-
vails throughout the scene. The size of the
screens fits this painting's subject.

Sansetsu reportedly made panel paintings of the same subject at the Kennin-ji and
Higashi Hongan-ji temples, but as those
panel paintings are no longer extant, these
screen paintings are all the more valuable.
Sansetsu emphasized the originality of the
Kanō school of Kyoto, which had a rival in
another Kanō school in Edo. Such intention
of his is well reflected in this work of art.

72
Genre Painting (Hikone Screen).

Six framed paintings.
Color on gold-foiled paper.
94.0 × 48.0cm (each).
Edo period, 17th century.
Ii-ke Hozonkai, Shiga.
National Treasure.

The right-hand side of the scene illustrates outdoor affairs whereas the left-hand side shows indoor affairs. The shift of scenes is expressed by using gold leaf. Today, these scenes are framed separately, but originally they were panels of one six-fold standing screen. The scene starts with a group of people showing their back and ends with another group of people also showing their back — which is a very intentional and dramatic composition. It is no over-statement to call this painting a prominent masterpiece not only among the genre paintings of the Edo period but also among those of the entire pre-modern ages.

Within this genre painting, there are depictions of stand-ing screens which in turn bear ink paintings. Because these ink paintings are so excellent, this genre painting is attri-buted to the Kanō school, though it has not been proved that a particular school produced it. This painting is ideal for providing a feeling for the atmosphere of one of the amusement sections in Kyoto in early Edo period (it does not seem to be the Shimabara licensed quarter, but Rokujō Misuji-chō). As the screen had been kept in the Ii family in Hikone, it is called "Hikone Byōbu" (Hikone Screen).

73
Screens of Pine Trees of Four Seasons.
By Kanō Tan'yū.

A pair of six-fold screens.
Color on gold-foiled paper.
156.5 × 367.0cm (each).
Edo period, 17th century.
Daitoku-ji temple, Kyoto.
Important Art Object.

Kanō Tan'yū had his residence in Edo (today's Tokyo), and as an official artist of the Tokugawa Shogunate he had latent power in the painting circle in the early Edo period. Nonetheless, Tan'yū was making lifelong efforts to improve his painting style.

In this painting, four pine trees are described in parallel on a pair of standing screens. By representing a single motif, i.e. pine trees, in different shapes and ages, the artist could express the four seasons. This is a notable example which indicates that Tan'yū was not only oriented towards Chinese style painting but also toward *Yamato-e* style Japanese painting. This technique of describing flowing water and this painting's composition on gold foiled paper clearly show that tendency. This is a work of Tan'yū when he was in his middle age, his so-called "Saigaki-age".

75
Five Hundred Rakan (Arhats).
By Ike-no-Taiga.

Eight hanging scrolls.
Light color on paper.
180.0 × 115.0cm (each).
Edo period, 18th century.
Mampuku-ji temple, Kyoto.
Important Cultural Property.

Ike-no-Taiga (1723–1776) had a long relationship with Mampuku-ji temple. At the age of seven, he made a large calligraphic work in front of the temple's Chinese abbot Kōdō and was praised as an infant prodigy.

The scrolls introduced here were originally sliding door-panel paintings, which were part of the panels Taiga painted in the Eastern *Hōjō* Hall in Mampuku-ji temple. Those panel paintings are assumed to have been made in 1765 on the occasion of abbot Taihō's retirement, but a more convincing opinion has emerged recently, saying that those paintings were made in 1772 at the 100th anniversary of Priest Ingen's death and as part of the Eastern *Hōjō* Hall's renovation. It has been suggested that the finger painting method may have been used for some part of the "Five Hundred Rakan (Arhats)", but it rather seems that the entire scene was painted by finger. ▶

73

75

76
Screens of Bamboo Trees.
By Maruyama Ōkyo.

A pair of six-fold screens.
Ink on paper.
160.3 × 353.3cm (each).
Edo period, dated 1776.
Enkō-ji temple, Kyoto.
Important Cultural Property.

It is known that these screens were produced in summer 1776 at Enkō-ji temple according to the inscriptions on the screens. Enkō-ji temple still owns these screens. At that time, Maruyama Ōkyo (1732–95) was forty-four years old. In the same year, he painted a screen of blooming wisteria in color on gold-foiled paper, combining the simplified brush strokes used for tree trunks with the minute expression of flowers and leaves. We can say that it was the year when Ōkyo's art began to flourish.

The right-hand screen represents a bamboo forest appearing dim in the rain, whereas the left-hand screen illustrates a different bamboo forest in a breeze; the two forests look a delicate contrast of rest and motion. The angles between the panels, which are a unique feature of standing screens, have been considered when the bamboos were arranged. The tasteful ink tone and cheerful brush strokes express these summertime bamboo forests very graciously.

77
Kanzan (Hanshan) and Jittoku
(Shide).
By Soga Shōhaku.

Two hanging scrolls.
Ink on paper.
197.0 × 115.0cm (each).
Edo period, 18th century.
Kōshō-ji temple, Kyoto.
Important Cultural Property.

Soga Shōhaku (1730–81) was considered insane during his life-time, but he himself seem to have been rather proud of that. He did his best in producing works of art which were different from other artists' works; that is to say that his works were full of originality.

Human figures were dashed onto the large, almost two meters long screens. They show some dignity and they look as if they scorned at our worldly thinking. These two paintings are filled with Shōhaku's originality. His attitude as an artist was much too eccentric for those days, during which the Kanō school was dominating the painting circle.

78
Ō Genshi (Wang Yuan-zhi)'s
Bamboo Hermitage.
By Tomioka Tessai.

Color on silk.
169.6 × 70.8cm.
Taishō period, dated 1917.
Kiyoshikōjin Seichō-ji temple, Hyogo.

The inscription is titled "Chikurō Fukyū" (The everlasting Bamboo Hermitage) in *Tensho* calligraphic style. It says: "The bamboo hermitage is very small and is located in the east of Fuzhi in Huang-zhou province. To the south of the hermitage is the Yang-zi River. It is a quiet and beautiful area and suitable for sail boats, fish and birds. According to *Ken-ki* (Jian-ji) record written by Wang Yuan-zhi in the Song dynasty, mountains are shining in the distance, the river is flowing near-by, and it is impossible to describe this elegant tranquility. The details are written in *Zhulou-ji* (Record of the Bamboo Hermitage), and therefore, I do not write too much here." Wang Yuan-zhi in the Song dynasty was in exile in Huang-zhou province and built two bamboo hermitages. After retiring from office, his constant companion was *Zhou Yi*, the book of philosophy, politics and the science of divination, and he liberated his mind from earthly thoughts by meditaing while being seated by the burning incense.

The composition of this painting has more depth and elaborateness than any other work of Tessai, who kept up the tradition of literati art throughout the Meiji and Taishō periods. The perfect harmony of his clear colors is excellent, too.

ROOM 12

Japanese culture was strongly influenced by Chinese culture before people turned their eyes toward the West. Even during the Heian period when the originality of Japanese culture was emphasized, the Japanese oriented themselves by referring to Chinese cultural activities. The popularity of ink paintings in the Muromachi period and Nanga paintings in the Edo period are the latest examples of Chinese influence.

In the old capital, Kyoto, many old Chinese paintings have been kept mainly in Zen temples. Most of them were brought to Japan by trading ships and visiting Buddhist priests between the Kamakura and Edo periods. Those paintings present Buddha, Maitreya (Miroku-bosatsu), Deva (Ten), Arhat (Rakan), Avalokiteśvara (Kannon-bosatsu) in white robe, Saints, the moment of spiritual Enlightenment of Zen priests and portraits of master priests. There were also landscape and flower-and-bird paintings of the Court style in the Southern Song dynasty, Zen art style paintings in the late Song and Yuan dynasties, and Zen school paintings in the Ming dynasty. Japanese not only appreciated those paintings from China, but also adopted some of their styles and techniques.

Kujaku Myō'ō
(Māyūra Vidyārāja).

Hanging scroll.
Color on silk.
167.1 × 102.6cm.
Northern Song dynasty, 11th century.
Ninna-ji temple, Kyoto.
National Treasure.

Myō'ō (Vidyārāja) in an unusual form is descending from Heaven, riding on a peacock and accompanied by clouds. Unlike the Japanese style Kujaku Myō'ō (Māyūra Vidyārāja), which usually has one face and four arms, this figure has three faces and six arms. In contrast to the central face, which has a merciful expression, the side faces look fierce.

The slender body is depicted with sharp lines from a slightly elevated view-point. Delicate shadings on the face indicate the intellectual coolness of this Myō'ō. The clothes and the whitish lotus seat are decorated minutely. The peacock, which is spreading its wings, is described very realistically and goes beyond iconographic expression.

In Ninna-ji temple, where this painting has been kept, the Buddhist ritual of Kujaku Myō'ō used to be performed. It is reported that Fujiwara Michinaga acquired an icon of Kujaku Myō'ō of the Tang dynasty, but later it was regrettably lost by fire.

80
Sixteen Rakan (Arhats).

Eight hanging scrolls from a set of sixteen.
Color on silk.
82.1 × 36.4cm (each).
Northern Song dynasty, 11th century.
Seiryō-ji temple, Kyoto.
National Treasure.

According to a recently stated and rather convincing opinion, these paintings are not the set of "Sixteen Rakan (Arhats)", which the Japanese Buddhist priest Chōnen brought to Japan from China. Rather, they are a different set of eighteen scrolls of Rakan paintings, from which two scrolls are missing. The painting style is remarkably classic for Rakan paintings of the Song dynasty. There are some aspects, which reveal the characteristics of Rakan paintings in Zengetsu style:

Figures are standing outdoors, surrounded by many rocks, and in many cases, close-ups of figures are showing grotesque features. However, the usage of thick colors and lines are entirely different from those of Zengetsu's Rakan paintings in the Imperial Collection. The eleventh figure is even depicted as a common Chinese Buddhist monk in Chōgen's style. The two styles of Zengetsu and Chogen are mixed in this set of paintings. Judging from the designs on the clothes, these paintings may have been made during the later Northern Song dynasty.

80

82
Autumn and Winter Landscapes.
Attributed to the Emperor Hui-zong.

Two hanging scrolls.
Color on silk.
128.2 × 55.2cm (each).
Southern Song dynasty, 12th century.
Konchi-in temple, Kyoto.
National Treasure.

Like the "Summer Landscape" kept in Kuon-ji temple in Yamanashi prefecture, each of these two scrolls bears two seals of Chinese collectors, "Zhong Ming Zhen-Wan" (Zhong Ming's rare articles) and "Lu-shi Jia Cang" (Lu Family property), and a third seal, "Tenzan", which indicates that the paintings were once owned by Yoshi-mitsu, the third Shogun of the Ashikaga clan. As all three landscape paintings bear the same set of seals and all of them are painted in the same style on silk, it can be assumed that these three paintings originally belonged to a set of four scrolls of the four seasons motif, from which the spring scroll is now missing.

Yoshitane, the tenth Shogun of the Ashikaga clan, gave these two scrolls to Mr. Ōuchi, who gave them to Sūden in Konchi-in temple via Myōchi-in temple. The two scrolls' limited subject matters and outstanding compositions which are based on the diagonal, neatly make the onlookers identify themselves with the human figures painted within the scenes, and they can experience the seasonal atmosphere. It seems that these scrolls were attributed to the Emperor Hui-zong after having been brought to Japan. The compositions of the paintings are similar to Ma Yuan's diagonal landscape style, while the texture painting is similar to Liang Kai's style. But since these scrolls show characteristics which precede the styles of Ma Yuan and Liang Kai, we can conclude that these scrolls were painted in the late twelfth century.

81
Landscape.
By Li Tang.

Two hanging scrolls.
Ink on silk.
66.5 × 43.6cm (each).
Southern Song dynasty, 12th century.
Kōtō-in temple, Kyoto.
National Treasure.

These two scrolls have been considered as the side scrolls from a set of three hanging scrolls with a painting of Kannon (Avalokiteśvara) as the central piece. They have been attributed to Wu Dao-zi. But recently a seal, saying "Painted by Li Tang", was discovered on these paintings, and since then these scrolls have been high-lighted as a work of Li Tang of the Southern Song dynasty.

There is an obvious contrast of seasons between the scroll of a boy carrying a big gourd bottle behind pine trees and the scroll of two human figures watching a waterfall, and when these two scrolls are placed side by side, they form one single large scene with a mountain in the center. These aspects indicate that originally these two scrolls belonged to a set of landscape paintings of four seasons. If there were four scrolls, it would be natural to think that the scroll with a boy represents summer and the scroll with a waterfall represents autumn. If these two scrolls are all by themselves from the beginning, then, the former scroll shows the scene from spring to summer and the latter show the scene from autumn to winter. Both of them were painted in Li Tang's new style, which excerted great influence on the Academy Paintings of the Southern Song dynasty. Simplified texture painting, which looks as if the ink was brushed off, is notable. Later, this style of texture painting was called "Dai Fuheki-shun" style.

83
Five Hundred Rakan (Arhats)
By Zhou Li-chang and Lin Ting-gui.

Hanging scroll from a set of eighty-two.
Color on silk.
110.3 × 52.7cm.
Southern Song dynasty, 12th century.
Daitoku-ji temple, Kyoto.
Important Cultural Property.

Five Rakan (Arhats) are painted on each scroll. Some of them are showing supernatural powers, and others are behaving as ordinary monks. Priest Yi-shao in Hui-an-yuan temple in the province of Ming-zhou (Ning-bo in Zhe-jian) raised funds and asked Zhou Li-chang and Lin Ting-gui to paint a set of five hundred Arhat figures. It took about ten years since 1178 to complete all the scrolls for the temple. This historical record and the names of donors are written in gold on the screens.

The painting styles can be roughly divided into two styles. The scrolls, in which faces are painted with sharp eyes and gorgeous colorings in pastel tints, were done by Lin Ting-gui and can clearly be distinguished from Zhou Li-chang's paintings. Zhou Li-chang's paintings are not mere Arhat painting but their nature is closer to genre paintings and portraits. One is impressed by the high standard of the civil Buddhist painters who were able to make paintings of various categories.

84
***Amida Jōdo-zu (Amitābha's
Paradise).***

Hanging scroll.
Color on silk.
148.5 × 92.3cm.
Southern Song dynasty, dated 1183.
Chion-in temple, Kyoto.
Important Cultural Property.

Bosatsu (Bodhisattva) and a Buddhist priest are placed on the clouds symmetrically above the standing Amida (Amitābha) triad, and a lotus pond is below the Amida triad. The nine figures kneeling on lotus seats on the pond and worshipping Amida represent nine classes of people in Amida's Paradise (Kubon Ōjō). Peacocks and cranes are painted around the pond as in flower-and-bird paintings. Though the composition is simple, without *Hōrō-kaku* pavillion nor stages, the scene maintains its lively atmosphere as all motifs which are painted in a stiff and strict shape are colored in gold and light tints. There is a horizontal seal at the lower right of the painting, indicating the date, though half of it is missing. This painting is an important work of standard Buddhist painting of the early Southern Song dynasty.

Seishi (Mahasthama-prapta)

85
Amida (Amitābha) Triad.
By Py-yue.

Three hanging scrolls.
125.6 × 48.6cm (Amida), 127.2 × 49.9cm
(Kannon), 127.3 × 48.8cm (Seishi).
Southern Song dynasty, 12th century.
Syōjōke-in temple, Kyoto.
Important Cultural Property.

Amida (Amitābha), Kannon (Avalokiteśvara), and Seishi (Mahās-thāma-prāpta) are painted as a triad on these three hanging scrolls. There is a seal at the top of each scroll, which reads "Si-ming Pu-yue". It is assumed that the artist, Pu-yue was from Si-ming (Ning-bo Zhe-jian), but nothing else is known about him.

Each figure of the triad is standing on lotus flowers and is surrounded by a vague and boat-shaped halo, which looks like the outer flame of a candle. Decoration in gold are arranged delicately in nice harmony with the elegant coloring with its subtly varying tones and strong strokes of lines in ink. This is a typical Buddhist painting of the Southern Song dynasty, which reflects the descent taste of the aristocracy.

87
Five Patriarchs of Jōdo Buddhism.

Hanging scroll.
Color on silk.
113.9 × 61.4cm.
Southern Song dynasty, 13th century.
Nison-in temple, Kyoto.
Important Cultural Property.

These portraits were reportedly brought to Japan from China by Priest Chōgen in 1168 on the request of Priest Hōnen, the founder of Japanese Jōdo Buddhism. The five figures are supposed to be Tang-luan (center), Dao-chuo (front, right), Shan-dau (front, left), Huai-gan (back, right), and Shao-kang (back, left).

However, as there is no established idea of five patriarchs of Jōdo Buddhism in China, which in fact was made up by Priest Hōnen himself, there is some doubt about the origin of this painting and about the identities of the five figures. Some art-historians think that these figures are five patriarchs of Zen Buddhism. The description of faces do not represent the personalities clearly, but the brush strokes are strict and clear and show the characteristics of the painting of the Southern Song dynasty well.

四
明
横
論
作
贊

嘉
定
三
秊
中
元

人
天
師
尊
不
容
贊
美

行
道
申
山
郎
傳
此
像

椎
笛
徐
儀
尤
䠞
扵
身

日
禪
日
教
無
非
為
人

泉
涌
寺
藏

(Dao-xuan)

86
Portraits of Priests
Dao-xuan
and Yuan-zhao.
Inscribed by Lou-yao.

Two hanging scrolls.
Color on silk.
171.0 × 81.7cm (each).
Southern Song dynasty, dated 1210.
Sennyū-ji temple, Kyoto.
Important Cultural Property.

Yu Xian, who was a leading figure in Hang-zhou Province, ordered these portraits. He also asked Lou Yao to add the inscription, and gave them to Priest Shunjō when Shunjō returned home. After his return to Japan, Priest Shunjō founded Sennyū-ji temple in Kyoto. The inscription by Lou Yao includes the date 1210, which was one year before the departure of Priest Shunjō.

Priest Xao-xuan of Nan-shan (596 - 667) is a founder of the Nan-shan-lu sect of Buddhism and was the most prominent scholar-priest during the Tang dynasty. Prist Yuan-zhao of Da-zhi (1948 - 1116) was a high priest during the Song dynasty, who contributed to the rivival of Buddhist precepts. In the painting Dao-xuan is holding a *Hossu*-brush, and Yuan-zhao is holding a scroll and a brush-pen. Both of them are sitting on *Kyokuroku* chairs, over which Buddhist robes are hung, and are facing each other obliquely. The contrast in the appearance of their faces is interesting. The fine designs of the robes reflect the sophisticated skill of the artist.

In 1227, another portrait of Priest Shunjō with an inscription by himself was completed, and since then, the three portraits have been kept as a set with the scroll of Priest Shunjō as a central piece.

88
Waterfall.

Hanging scroll.
Ink on silk.
64.5 × 103.2cm.
Southern Song dynasty, 13th century.
Chishaku-in temple, Kyoto.
Important Cultural Property.

This painting is said to have been captioned by Sōami as "Waterfall by Wang Mo-jie in the Tang dynasty". The top of the waterfall is described from a short distance and the simple scene is composed of only water and rocks.

Mist is painted in light ink at the top of the scene, and splashes of water are depicted over the waterfall's basin. The descriptions of falling water and rough water are far removed from realism, being rather patternized. Strokes of the flat brush-pen are often used for the depiction of rocks at both sides of the painting. Though the artist mainly used the *Dai Fuheki-shun* (Da Fupi-zhou) texture painting style, which was invented by Li Tang, he was able to avoid monotony.

The description of transforming water in ink has a long history in Chinese painting since the period of the Five Dynasties, and Ma Yuan painted a masterpiece, during the Southern Song dynasty, under the title "Twelve Variations of Water". The soft lines of this waterfall painting are based on this tradition, but the painting is more elegant.

90
Wizards Toad and Tie-guai.
By Yan-hui.

Two hanging scrolls.
Color on silk.
161.3 × 79.7cm (each).
Yuan dynasty, 14th century.
Chion-ji temple, Kyoto.
Important Cultural Property.

Two wizards, Liu Hai-chen, who was often called "Wizard of Toad" and Li Tie-guai, are sitting on rocks as if they were talking to each other. Li Tie-guai, whose iron cane is leaning against his breast, is blowing off his soul from his body. His body, now without soul, began to change its color and cadaveric rigidity was taking hold. Liu Hai-chan is holding a peach, which symbolizes eternal youth and longevity, and has a big white toad sitting on his shoulder.

Yan-hui (Qui-yue) from Lu-ling (today's Ji-an in Jian-xi), who painted these scrolls, was active during the late thirteenth century as a painter of Taoist and Buddhist figures. A new modeling sense, which was different from the realistic expression in the Song dynasty, is evident in the deformed facial expressions, which emphasize the grotesque motif, and in the boldly winding drapes of the clothes.

89
Court Lady.

Hanging scroll.
Color on silk.
86.4 × 30.0cm.
Yuan dynasty, 13th century.
National Treasure.

A court lady in male attire with a flute in her belt is staring at her finger tips and is lost in thoughts. Her black satin cap bears a design of flowers. She wears a gold-wire bracelet around her wrist. She is slightly raising her arm and puts the finger tips of both hands together. It is the very posture of a young lady.

Wearing male attire was fashionable among court ladies in China, especially during the Tang dynasty, and there are some wall-paintings describing such figures. This painting is a descendant of the beauty paintings of the Tang dynasty. There is one article among the essays written during the Song dynasty, which introduced a painting of a court lady made during the period of the Five Dynasties by Zhou Wen-ju, who succeeded the painting style of beautiful ladies of the Tang dynasty. The description of that painting in the article coincides with the composition of this painting of a court lady.

The seal of another artist by the name of Qian Xuan was stamped onto this painting. It was added later, but the date of production of this painting falls into the period of Qian Xuan's career as an artist. Some people think that the model of this court lady was Huan Yi (Shu-wong), who was a master player of the flute during the Eastern Jin dynasty; this painting was therefore sometimes called "Portrait of Huan Shu-wang", but it is hard to support this idea.

91
Album of Kannon
(Avalokiteśvara).
By Chen Xian.

Album.
Light color on satin.
35.5 × 53.7cm (each).
Ming dynasty, dated 1636.
Mampuku-ji temple, Kyoto.
Important Cultural Property.

Eighteen figures of Kannon (Avalokiteśvara) are painted in this album. Kannon's drapes are depicted by gentle but accentuated ink lines. The shading of faces is expressed in light colors which creates a three dimentional effect on the faces. Priest Ingen, who established the Ōbaku sect of Zen Buddhism in Japan, added an inscription to each painting.

Chen Xian, who was active in Fu-jian Province, was an artist of Buddhist paintings, and many of his works were included in the Buddhist paintings which Zen monks of the Ōbaku sect brought to Japan. These Kannon figures were painted by Chen Xian in 1636 at Kai-yuan-si temple at Mt. Zi-yun in Fu-jian according to the inscription of the 18th painting of this album.

ROOM 13

Calligraphy, which developed as a visual art in China, Korea and Japan is exhibited in this room. Chinese and Korean collections range from the rubbings made of some monuments in ancient days to the relatively new ones in the Ming and Qing dynasties in China and Yi dynasty in Korea. Japanese collections range from old pieces of the Nara period to those in the Edo period. Old records and documents are also exhibited once in a while.

Chinese characters which were originally hieroglyphs had a latent possibility to become art from the beginning. When paper and brush pens were invented, calligraphy as a category of visual art was established.

The Japanese made up their original *Kana* letters based on Chinese characters, and considered the calligraphy of both languages as visual art. Several different styles of *Kana* letters were invented and these helped to form distinctive Japanese calligraphic styles.

92
Dai Hannya-kyō sutra (Mahāprajñāpāramitā sutrta).
Ordered by King Nagaya.

One folio volume from a set of 142 volumes.
Ink on paper.
23.8 × 8.7cm (each).
Nara period, dated 712.
Taihei-ji temple, Shiga.
National Treasure.

King Nagaya, who is famous for his revolution, ordered the duplication of the first section of the *Dai Hannya-kyō* sutra (Mahāprajñāpāramitā sutra) twice — in 712 and in 719; The *Dai Hannya-kyō* sutra consists of six hundred volumes. These folio volumes contain the surviving parts of the first duplication, which was meant as a prayer on behalf of the late Emperor Mommu, who had died on June 15, 707. This duplicated sutra is known as "Wadō-kyō" (sutra in the Wadō era). The text of the sutra was duplicated neatly in the calligraphic style for sutras of the Sui dynasty in China. Hemp paper was used, and there is no partition of the paper. This duplication is representative for the early Nara period.

King Nagaya is known to have been a son of Prince Takaichi, but according to the notes added to this duplicated sutra, King Nagaya was called "His Imperial Highness Nagaya" and "Prince of the Northern Palace". These notes offer valuable information about the circumstances in those days.

It is amazing that as many as 142 volumes of the sutra are still extant, all of which have been kept in Taihei-ji temple. This duplicated sutra was originally written on handscrolls, but later on, these handscrolls were bound into folio volumes.

93
List of Objects Brought to Japan by Priest Kōbō.
By Priest Saichō.

Ink on paper.
27.1 × 885.0cm.
Early Heian period, 9th century.
Kyō'ō-gokoku-ji temple, Kyoto.
National Treasure.

This list is a register of objects which Priest Kūkai (Kōbō-daishi, 774-835) brought to Japan from China during the Tang dynasty. The objects included Buddhist texts and studies of sutras, etc., and were dedicated to the Emperor Heijō in October, 806. From the handwriting, it is clear that Priest Saichō (Dengyō-daishi, 767-822) wrote it.

It is said that Priest Saichō copied the list from the original, which had been written by Priest Kūkai. It is assumed that this list had originally been kept in Enryaku-ji temple, as the red square seal "Hieizan-in" (seal of the temple on Mt. Hiei) is stamped over all the joints of the list's seventeen sheets.

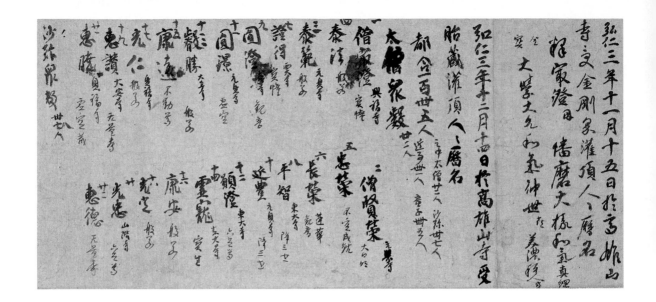

94
Record of the Kanjō Baptism.
By Priest Kūkai.

Ink on paper.
28.8 × 266.1cm.
Early Heian period, 9th century.
Jingo-ji temple, Kyoto.
National Treasure.

This record is a list of people who received the *Kanjō* baptism, which was administered by Priest Kūkai (Kōbō-daishi, 767-822) at Takaosan-ji (today's Jingo-ji temple) three times between 812 and 813. Hundred and sixty-six people, including both Buddhist priests and common citizens, were baptized. Priest Saichō (Dengyō-daishi) was among them. The names were written separately on each of the three occasions; calligraphic styles and script types of the corresponding sections differ slightly from each other. Although this record was written in haste, the brush strokes are strong and Kūkai's calligraphic characteristics are more evident in this piece than in any other of his works.

This volume had been transfered from Jingo-ji temple to Ninna-ji temple at some earlier date, but the Emperor Go-Uta transfered it back to Jingo-ji temple in 1308.

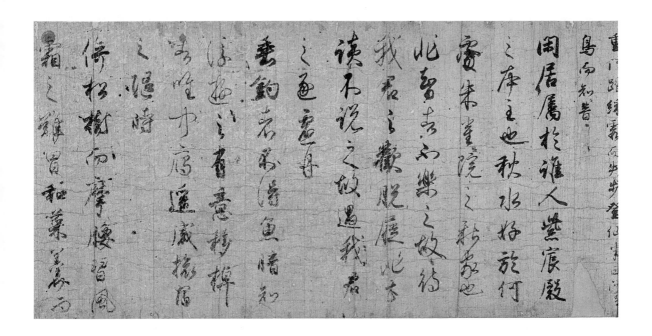

95
Calligraphic Volume.
By Fujiwara Yukinari.

Ink on paper.
29.4 × 188.2cm.
Late Heian period, 11th century.
Honnō-ji temple, Kyoto.
National Treasure.

This volume is a segment of a handscroll which contains duplicates of poems by Sugawara Michizane, Kino Haseo, and others. As it has been kept in Honnō-ji temple, it is called "Honnō-ji gire".

The name of the calligrapher is not given, but based on comparisons with other works, it is assumed that Fujiwara Yukinari (972-1027), one of the three master calligraphers, wrote it. Four sheets of paper with printed decorations of vines and phoenixes are attached to each other to form this scroll. Judging from the gorgeous paper and the talented calligrapher, this scroll is considered to have been made as a calligraphic example for aristocrats.

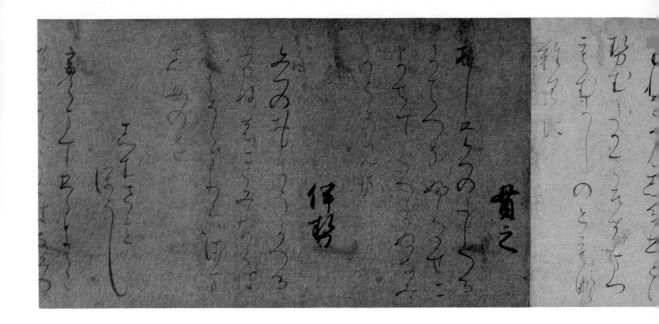

97
Hokekyō Sutra in Gold on Purple Paper.

Including Opening and Closing sutras.
Handscroll from a set of ten scrolls.
Gold on purple paper.
26.5 × 983.4cm (Vol. I).
Late Heian period, 12th century.
Hompō-ji temple, Kyoto.
Important Cultural Property.

This is an extant section of the ten volumes of the complete *Hokekyō* sutra, which consists of the eight volumes of the main text, one volume of *Muryōgi-kyō* (Opening sutra) and one volume of *Kanfuken-kyō* (Closing sutra). It is reportedly attributed to Ono-no-Tōfū, but the date of production is assumed to have been between the late 11th and the early 12th centuries. There are many extant sutras written in gold on dark blue paper, but this sutra, written in gold on purple paper, is a rare object, and its descent *Wayō*-style handwriting is outstanding. The purple color has faded and there are some damages at the beginning and end of the scroll, but nonetheless, it is a precious sutra volume, as it has survived as a complete scroll with handwriting in gold on purple paper.

The sutra case with its mother-of-pearl-inlaid decoration of *Hōsōge* flowers is extant, too. Both the sutra and the sutra case were donated to the temple by Hon'ami Kōetsu (1558-1637). The donor's letter written by Kōetsu has been kept together with the sutra. This sutra volume was repaired recently and is now mounted as a thick scroll.

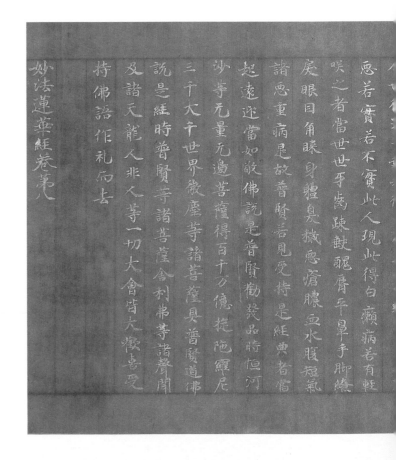

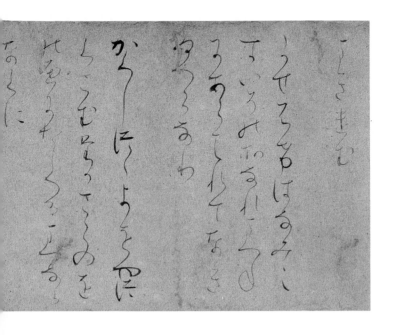

96
Kokin Waka-shū Anthology of Poems.
Manshu-in Version.

Ink on paper.
14.1 × 285.5cm.
Late Heian period, 12th century.
Manshu-in temple, Kyoto.
National Treasure.

This is a segment of the *Kokin Waka-shū* anthology of poems, which has been kept in Manshu-in temple. Thirty-one poems from the chapter of "Miscellaneous Poems" in the seventeenth volume are covered by this volume. Seven sheets of dyed paper — in indigo, light blue, and light red colors — are attached so as to form an elegant scroll. The script style is a graceful mixture of the female style and the grass style. According to one report, this scroll is attributed to Fujiwara Yukinari (972-1027), but the handwriting does not resemble his. It is assumed that this scroll was originally made as a calligraphic example.

Fujiwara Tsugizane wrote a brief history of this scroll at the end of this volume. It was given by the ex-Emperor Sutoku to Bishop Shōji and then given to the wife of Fujiwara Tsugizane.

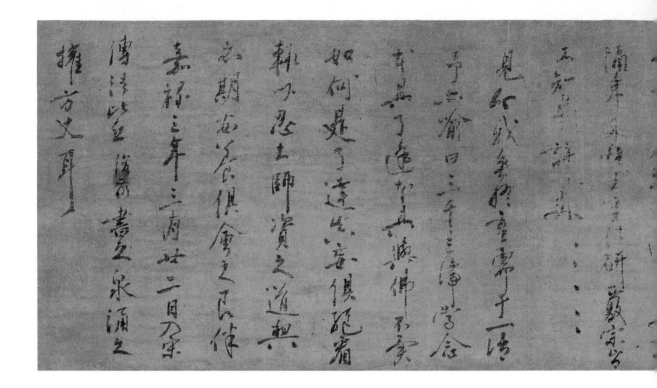

99
Certificate "Fuhō-jō„
By Priest Shunjō

Ink on paper.
33.6 × 98.5cm.
Kamakura period, dated 1227.
Sennyū-ji temple, Kyoto.
National Treasure.

This certificate was given by Priest Shunjō, who founded Sennyū-ji temple, to his successor, Priest Shinkai, when Shunjō realized that he would soon die. "Fuhō-jō" certifies that his disciple has mastered the grand prayer and the secret prayer.

Priest Shunjō was from Higo (today's Kumamoto prefecture). He was a well-known scholar-priest who had mastered the Buddhist ideas of the eight major Buddhist sects. He went to China in 1199 during the Song dynasty and returned to Japan after thirteen years of studying there. He founded Sennyū-ji temple in 1218 in the Higashiyama area in Kyoto. Though this certificate was written when he had been sick in bed, the elegant calligraphic style of Shunjō, who practiced the style of Huang Shan-gu (Ting-jian) of the Northern Song Dynasty, is evident.

98
Nihon Ryōi-ki.

Vols. II and III from a set of three volumes.
Ink on paper.
25.6 × 14.2cm.
Late Heian period, 12th century.
Raigō-in temple, Kyoto.
National Treasure.

This scroll is a duplicate of the oldest Buddhist stories, *Nihon Ryōi-ki*, written by Priest Keikai. Another duplicate of the same text, which was copied during the mid-Heian period, has been kept in Kōfuku-ji temple, But since the Kōfuku-ji duplicate covers only the first volume of the text, this scroll in Raigō-in temple must be considered as the oldest extant duplicate of the second and the third volumes of the text.

The text is bound in the style of a book. *Hishi* paper without partition is used. Introductions are added to both the first and the second volumes. This duplicated book is very highly valued in the history of Japanese literature.

当者香尘心海开等于战阳教
初习开名访道游游边苏求
我以来将超死生乘之以一
乘围顿之道于元其汹如
之郡性化海一叶以甘露心
园意解三昧政海山枚
千里之缘本华三赋漾漾

99

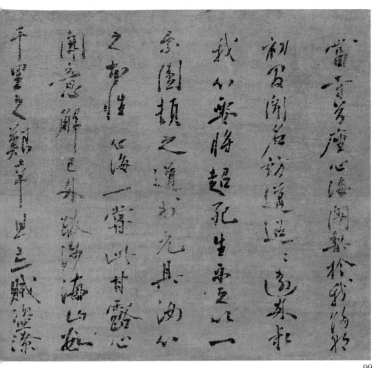

98

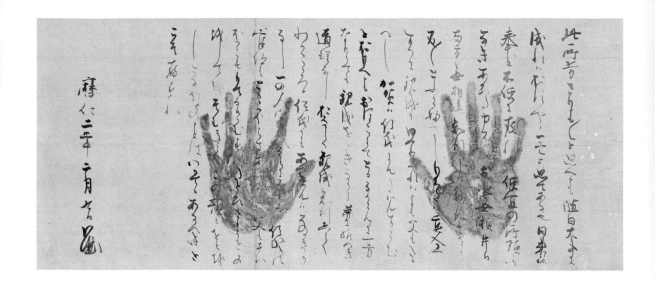

100
Emperor Go-Toba's
Autograph Will with His Hand-
prints.

Ink on paper.
30.9 × 101.2cm.
Kamakura period, dated 1239.
Minase shrine, Osaka.
National Treasure.

Ex-Emperor Go-Toba (1180-1239) was exiled to Oki island after his defeat at the Battle of Jōkyū. This is his autograph will, which he wrote for his faithful retainer Fujiwara (Minase) Chikanari about ten days before his death. The will states that the estates in Settsu (some parts of today's Osaka and Hyōgo prefectures) and in Izumo (today's Shimane prefecture) were to be given to Chikanari.

Wishing that his will be fulfilled, the ex-Emperor sealed this document with both of his palms in red ink. While he was dying in exile, ex-Emperor Go-Toba was anxious about his loyal retainer's future before anything else. His hand-prints even have a touch of grimness.

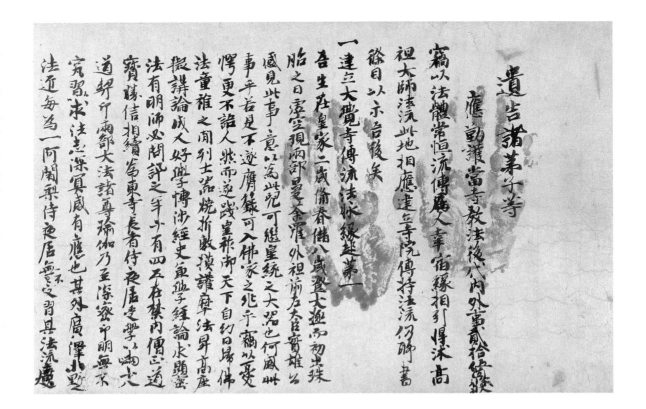

101
***Emperor Go-Uda's Autograph
Will with His Hand-prints.***

Ink on paper.
54.5 × 788.8cm.
Kamakura period, 14th century.
Daikaku-ji temple, Kyoto.
National Treasure.

This is the written will of Emperor Go-Uda (1267-1324) in which he expressed his wish for the prosperity of Daikaku-ji temple. Following Priest Kūkai's written will, Emperor Go-Uda intended to write a will of twenty-five articles, but for some reasons the will was completed with only twenty-one articles.

This document is considered to have been an original draft of the will, because there are correction marks at some places. However, the Emperor's hand prints are stamped over the first seven articles, which expresses the Emperor's earnest wish. Therefore, there is no doubt that this scroll became the official written will of the Emperor, although, it originally had been a draft. It is also possible that the Emperor was not able to complete his draft by his death in June, 1324 and that this document has been kept as his written will.

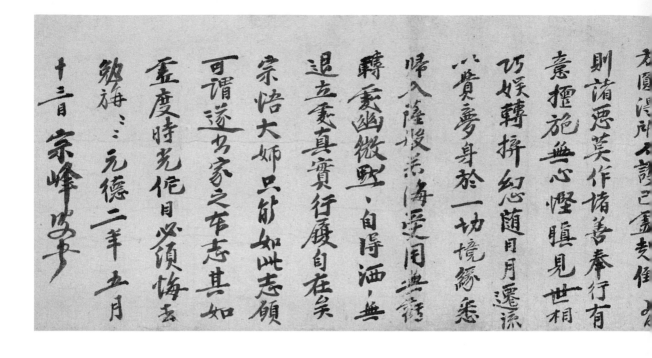

102
Calligraphy by Priest
Daitō-kokushi.
Buddhist lesson to Sōgo Daishi.

Ink on paper.
32.4 × 135.4cm.
Kamakura period, dated 1330.
Daisen-in temple, Kyoto.
National Treasure.

Priest Daitō-kokushi (Shūhō Myōchō, 1282-1337), who is famous for establishing Daitoku-ji temple, was from Harima (today's Hyōgo prefecture) and entered into priesthood at the age of eleven. He studied Buddhism in the Tendai sect, but he later converted and studied under Priest Kōhō Kennichi. In autumn 1305 he visited Priest Nampo Jōmyō, who had started the Daiō school, and passed the "Un'mon-no-Seki" examination (test at the gate of cloud) and acquired the certificate under Jōmyō's supervision. People of the high society respected him. Ex-Emperor Hanazono invited him for his instruction in Zen Buddhism and bestowed the title "Kozen Daitō-kokushi" on him. After listening to his preaching, the Emperor Go-Daigo bestowed another title, "Kōshō Shōtō-kokushi", on him.

This scroll is a Buddhist lesson explaining Buddhist life, which transcends both earthly life and death, and was given to Sōgo Taishi. Twenty-six lines of the text are written on the three sheets of paper, which are attached to each other. This scroll is one of the most excellent pieces among Daitō-kokushi's autograph texts. It is part of the *Daitō-kokushi Shūi-roku* (Collected works of Priest Daitō-kokushi).

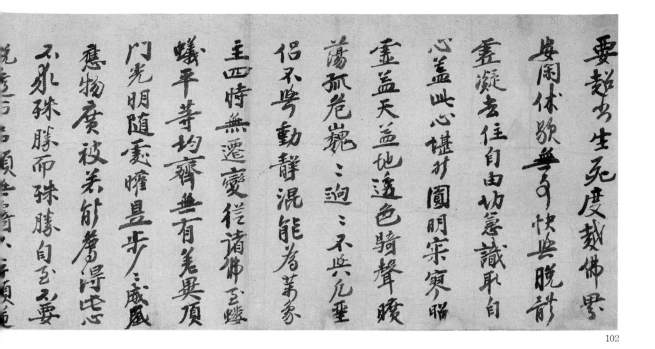

要超出生死度裁佛累
毋閑休頼無了快其脱龍
靈凝去住自由功意識取自
心蓋此心諶才圓明宗寒照
靈蓋天蓋地遠色騎聲暖
蕩孤危巉巉迥不與兀坐
侣不學動静混能卷茅蓋
主四特無遷愛徃諸佛玉蝶
蟻平等均齊無有差異頂
門光明隨處幢畢步感風
應物廣被若射箭得忠
不外殊勝而殊勝自己不要

102

諸山眾審等持明與和尚
禪師榮庸
命遷良
演法禪寺開卷
乗我手同照
合洞筋
駕者
右伏必萬年松径
匹書靈後孫等
景代人久自足
年束益著諸
山有行星四漢同
幢恭惟
新命兵如堂上明興
和為禪師行脚
跨滄溪親見
中峯挺霓雪決眥
小天下必教止脉

103

103
*Calligraphy by Priest
Jikusen Bonsen.*
**Shozanso Greetings to Priest
Meisō Seitetsu.**

Ink on silk.
39.1 × 145.4cm (each).
Namboku-chō period, 14th century.
Ryūkō-in temple, Kyoto.
National Treasure.

These are scrolls of *Shozanso* greetings, which Priest Jikusen Bonsen (Du-xian Feng-qian) wrote, when Priest Meisō Seitetsu entered Shinnyo-ji temple as an abbot. *Shozanso* are greetings extended to a newly appointed abbot from other abbots of the same school. Priest Mutoku Shinkō of Ankoku-ji temple, Priest Kōzan Sōshō of Manju-ji temple, Priest Kozan Ikkyō of Tōfuku-ji temple, Priest Mugaku Shigen of Tenryū-ji temple, and Priest Mōzan Chimyō of Nanzen-ji temple signed these greetings. Priest Bonsen was from Xiang-shan prefecture of the Ming Province (today's Zhe-jiang province) and was a successor of Priest Kurin Seimu. Bonsen came to Japan in 1329 and was consecutively serving as the abbot of Kenchō-ji and Jōchi-ji temples in Kamakura and Nanzen-ji and Shinnyo-ji temples in Kyoto. These wide *Shozanso* scrolls are written with vigorous brush strokes in the *Sōsho* (grass) and the *Gyōsho* calligraphic styles.

Priest Meisō Seitetsu was the successor of Priest Chūhō Myōhon (Zhong-feng Ming-ben) of the temple on Mt. Tian-mu. Seitetsu went to China in 1318 during the Yuan dynasty and returned to Japan in 1326. Saitetsu and Bonsen were friends and sometimes exchanged poems.

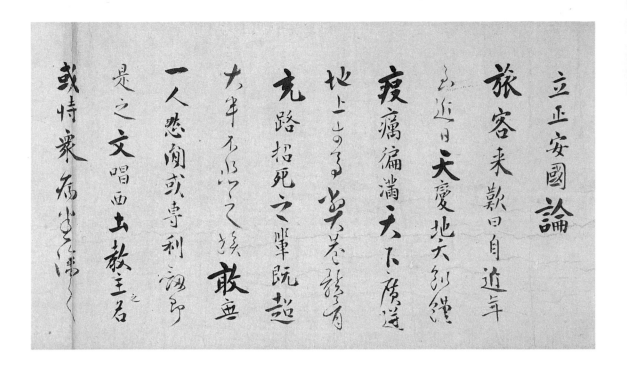

立正安國論

旅客来歎曰自近年

至近日天變地夭相續

疫癘偏滿天下廣迸

地上之牛半斃有

充路招死之輩既超

大半不冕之族敢無

一人悲闷或專利劍印

是之文唱土教主名

或特衆為生死傷

104
Risshō Ankoku-ron.
Duplicated by Hon'ami Kōetsu.

Ink on paper.
39.1 × 351.0cm.
Momoyama period, dated 1619.
Myōren-ji temple, Kyoto.
Important Cultural Property.

Hon'ami Kōetsu (1558-1637) duplicated this text on the recommendation by Priest Nichigen of Myōren-ji temple in Kyoto. According to the postscript, the date of production was 1619, when Kōetsu was 62 years old. The characteristic calligraphic style of Kōetsu, who was one of the three master calligraphers during the Kan'ei era (1624-1644), is evident.

Risshō Ankoku-ron is a text written by Priest Nichiren in the style of questions and answers. He sent it to Regent Hōjo Tokiyori, emphasizing the importance of propagating the orthodox ideas of the *Hokekyō* sutra. Kōetsu was a pious Buddhist of the Hokke sect, and he duplicated another Buddhist text, the *Shibun Butsujō-gi* in Myōren-ji temple, on the request of Priest Nichigen.

105
Bosatsu Shotai-kyō Sutra.

From the set of five volumes.
Ink on paper.
24.1 × 9.2cm (each).
West Wei dynasty, dated 550.
Chion-in temple, Kyoto.
National Treasure.

The original title is "Bosatsu-jūtojutsu Tengojin Motaisetsu Kōfu-kyō" sutra, which was translated into Chinese by Priest Du Fu-nian during the Late Qin dynasty. This sutra focuses on the life of Buddha before and after his "nirvana" or final enlightenment. During that period, Buddha was in a Mother's womb for ten month and was preaching to several Bosatsu (Bodhisattvas). The first volume of this set of five volumes was duplicated in the late Heian period, and the fifth volume was duplicated in the Nara period. The three other volumes are dated 550 in the Chinese calendar. According to their post-scripts, these three volumes are the surviving volumes of the *Issai-kyō* sutras (whole Buddhist scriptures), which were duplicated on the request of thirty persons, including Tao Wu-hu at Tao-lan-si temple. They are the oldest extant volumes of *Bosatsu Shotai-kyō* sutra, which are clearly dated and have been handed down from generation to generation. The keen calligraphic style of these three volumes, which were influenced by the Northern Dynasty's calligraphy, is excellent. The third volume, which is a significant object in the history of old duplicated sutras, was part of the masterpiece-collection of Priest Ugai Tetsujō (the 75th abbot of Chion-in temple), who was a well-known collector of old sutras.

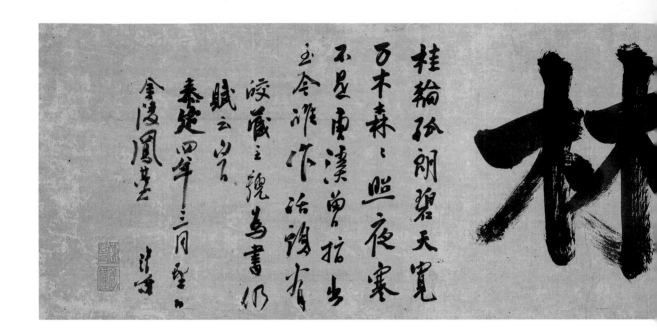

108
Calligraphy by Priest Gu-lin
Qing-mao.
"Getsurin".

Ink on paper.
36.4 × 120.3cm.
Yuan dynasty, dated 1327.
Chōfuku-ji temple, Kyoto.
National Treasure.

"Getsurin" is the title which Priest Gu-lin Qing-mao (1262-1329) bestowed on the Japanese Priest Dōkō Zōsu in 1327. Priest Dōkō (1293-1351) came to Priest Gu-lin of Bao-ning-si temple on Mt. Feng-tai in Jin-ling in spring, 1322 during the Yuan dynasty and became Gu-lin's disciple. After nine years of study under Priest Gu-lin, Dōkō became the head disciple and was bestowed the title "Getsurin". After Gu-lin's death, Dōkō returned to Japan in 1330. Later, in Japan, supported by Kiyokage, the feudal lord of Umezu during the Rekiō era (1338-42), Dōkō transformed a convent of the Tendai sect into a Zen temple and thus became the founder of Chōfuku-ji Zen temple.

Priest Gu-lin was from Wen Province (today's Zhe-jian province) and was a successor of Priest Hen-chuan Ru-gong. The title "Getsurin" on the scroll was written two years before his death. The vigorous calligraphy reflects his personality.

108

106
Kongō-kyō (Vajra-sutra).
Duplicated by Zhang Ji-zhi.

Ink on paper.
32.1 × 12.5cm.
Southern Song dynasty, dated 1253.
Chishaku-in temple, Kyoto.
National Treasure.

This sutra, originally titled "Kongō Hannya Haramitsu-kyō", was duplicated by Zhang Ji-zhi (1186-1266), who was a representative master calligrapher in the Southern Song dynasty in China. According to the postscript, it was duplicated on July 13, 1253, when Ji-zhi was at the age of sixty-eight, in commemoration of his deceased mother; in the followig year, Ji-zhi donated the sutra to Zen Priest Xi-yan, who was the senior monk in Jing-de Zen temple at Mt. Tian-tong in China. Being a pious Buddhist, Zhang Ji-zhi duplicated the *Kongō-kyō* sutra many times. His calligraphic style with large characters for which he had a special talent, and his prudent brush strokes are evident in this work. The calligraphy of Zhang Ji-zhi, together with that of Hung Ting-jian in the Northern Song dynasty and Zhang Zi-ang in the Yuan dynasty, excerted considerable influence on the Zen calligraphy in Japan during the Kamakura peirod.

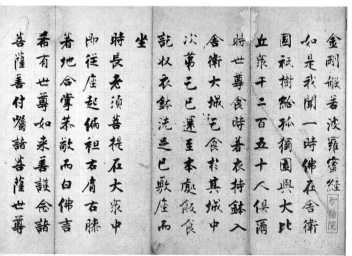

106

107
Calligraphic Frames and Plates
for Zen Temples.

From the collection of 14 frames
and 5 plates.
Ink on paper.
44.8 × 92.3cm.
Southern Song dynasty, 13th century.
Tōfuku-ji temple, Kyoto.
National Treasure.

Many original calligraphic works for the frames and plates of Zen temples have been kept in Tōfuku-ji temple, one of the five major temples in Kyoto. The calligraphic works in Tōfuku-ji temple were originally given to Shōten-ji temple in Hakata by Priest Bujun Shiban (Zen Priest Butsugan, 1186-1266), who was the master of Priest Enni Bennen (Shōichi-kokushi, 1202-1280), the founder of Shōten-ji temple. When Shōten-ji temple was attacked by Tendai sect monks, Priest Enni and these calligraphic pieces took refuge in Tōfuku-ji temple, which has also been founded by Priest Enni. Since then, these calligraphic pieces have been kept in Tōfuku-ji temple. All of the calligraphies are written in large-size letters, and judging from the calligraphic styles, not only Priest Bujun but also Zhang Ji-zhi, a talented calligrapher in the Southern Song dynasty, who was familiar with Zen temples, may have written them. Brush strokes are vigorous and strong, and the calligraphers' spirit can be felt in the grave atmosphere of the works. Among them, this calligraphic piece introduced in this article shows Zhang Ji-zhi's calligraphic style. The written word "Shuso" is a status title for Zen monks, meaning the head of all the monks.

ROOM 14

Textile art objects have been produced in several areas in the world since the beginning of civilization. Those textile art objects, such as clothings, originally made for practical use, but later on, decorative aspects were added. As soon as decorativeness became one of the elements of textile art, different costume styles and techniques developed according to geographical area, era, and purpose.

In Room 14, oriental textile art objects of mainly Japanese and Chinese origin, ranging from ancient times to the modern ages, are exhibited. Among those oriental textile works are many Japanese and Chinese textile masterpieces entrusted to our museum by temples and shrines. They consist of Buddhist costumes brought to Japan by Priest Kūkai and Priest Saichō, Kumano Hayatama Shrine's old treasures, which reflect the elegant taste of court nobles, and gorgeous *Kosode* style dresses of the Momoyama and Edo periods. These exhibits are a record of the development of Chinese and Japanese textile works.

Thematic displays assembled from museum collections and entrusted objects are replaced every one or two months. Sometimes, the development of techniques of textile art is focused on, while some other times the meaning of motifs of textile art objects is highlighted. Sometimes, costumes used in temples or shrines for religious purposes are exhibited, and sometimes costumes for the performing arts are displayed. Characteristics of the costumes of different social classes and the relationship between clothings and the seasons are also shown. The displays are organized in a way which makes the role of textile art in people's life and culture observable.

On the occasion of the Plum Festival (dolls' festival), dolls such as *Hina* and *Gosho* dolls are on display. Other special displays are held on several occasions.

109
Kenda-kokushi Kesa-robe.

Silk brocade.
116.8 × 237.0cm.
Tang dynasty, 8th century.
Kyō'ō-gokoku-ji temple, Kyoto.
National Treasure.

This Buddhist *Kesa*-robe was reportedly given by Priest Hui-quo to Priest Kūkai, while Kūkai was studying in China during the Tang dynasty, and it is registered in *Goshōrai Mokuroku*, which is a list of objects which Priest Kūkai brought to Japan. "Kenda" is said to indicate the yellowish-red color used for the robe, and "Kokushi" means "brocade".

The central "Densō" part of the robe is woven with threads of about ten different colors such as purple, "moegi" bluish-yellow, yellow and indigo, to form a brocaded pattern of clouds. There are some parts, which look as if they were stitched with purple threads, but they, too, are woven patterns. These cloud-patterns and purple stitch patterns imitate the stains of *Funzō-e* robes, which were the original form of the *Kesa*-robes that had been made of washed waste-rag pieces. In an elaborate manner, excellent brocade is made to have the appearance of waste-rags.

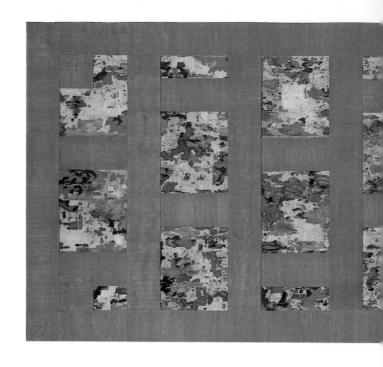

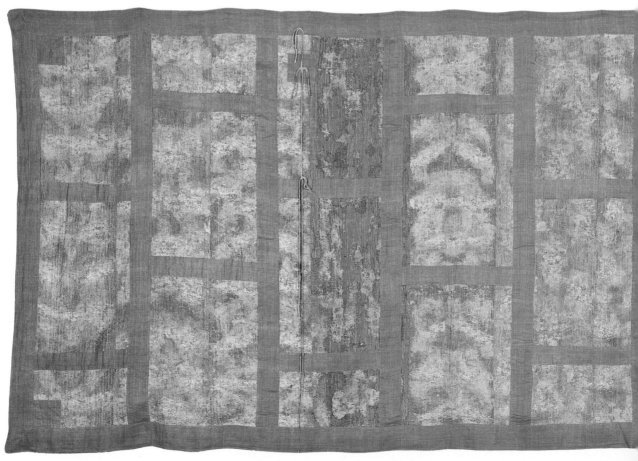

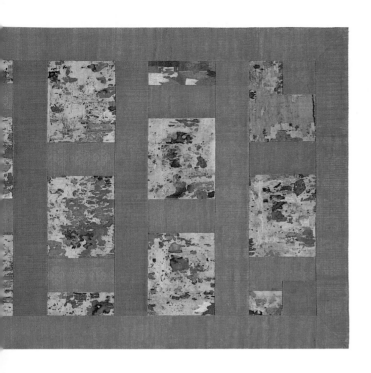

110
Shichijō Shinō Kesa-robe.

Quilted hemp.
132.0 × 260.0cm.
Tang dynasty, 8th century.
Enryaku-ji temple, Shiga.
National Treasure.

It is reported that this Buddhist *Kesa*-robe was originally owned by Priest Jin-xi (Priest Zhan-ran, the sixth patriarch of Chinese Tendai Buddhism, 711-782). The robe was handed down from Jin-xi's disciple, Priest Xing-man of Fu-long-si temple at Mt. Tian-tai, to his Japanese disciple Priest Saichō. In the *Gokyōzō Hōmotsu Shogyō-tō Mokuroku* (list of temple treasures and Buddhist texts), which Saichō compiled before his death in 811, one *Kesa*-robe, called "Keikei-wajō (Priest Jin-xi) Butsurō-zō (kept in Fu-long-si temple) "Fuhō Kesa Chinō" is registered along with other objects. That robe in the list is considered to be *Shichijō Shinō Kesa*, which is being introduced in this article. "Chinō" means "patching of hemp strips". On the central "Densō" part of this robe, hemp fibers of various colors such as white, dark blue, brown, red, etc. and purple hemp strips were placed on a coarse hemp fabric and were quilted. Following the original form of *Funzō-e* robe, which used to be made of patched rags, this robe was made of quilted hemp fabric. Its characteristic point is that hemp fibers are used together with other materials for quilting.

111
Ōhi-robe with Sammen-hōju and Katsuma Design.

Brocade.
79.4 × 227.0cm.
Kamakura period, 13th century.
Ninna-ji temple, Kyoto.
Important Cultural Property.

Ōhi Buddhist robe covers the right shoulder of a priest, who is wearing a *Shichijō-gesa* robe. According to the temple record, this *Ōhi*-robe was originally owned by the temple's second abbot, Priest Shōshin (1005-85), during the Heian period.

The designs of *Sammen-hōju* and *Katsuma* were woven by the *Nuki-nishiki* method, using monochrome warps for the background and wefts of several colors for the designs. This method has been used since the Heian period, but unlike *Nuki-nishiki* brocades of the Heian period, which depict gentle designs and colors, this brocade shows a clear contrast between the dark-blue background and red flames, and, nonetheless, creates a calm atmosphere. *Hōju* magic balls and flames are depicted with sharp lines. When considering of these charcteristics of the brocade, it seems that this brocade was woven during the Kamakura period.

112
Akome Wear with Designs of Small Hollyhocks, Butterflies and Circles.
Ueno-Hakama-trousers with Designs of Camellia and Vines.

Old shrine treasures.
Length: 108.3cm (Ueno Hakama).
Length: 176.0cm, Sleeve length: 82.7cm (Akome).
Namboku-chō period, ca. 1390.
Kumano Hayatama shrine, Wakayama.
National Treasure.

Kumano Hayatama shrine in Shingū city in Wakayama prefecture has been keeping many old treasures donated in 1390 and thereafter by the Imperial Palace, the Sentō Palace, the Shogun's Muromachi Palace and the government officials of various provinces. The major objects of those treasures are lacquered works, such as hand-boxes and Shintoist costumes. Those Shintoist costumes reflect the formal fashion of court nobles in the Middle Ages. Elegant fabrics for court nobles (Yūsoku-ori), such as double-fold fabrics, float-weave, solid-twill, etc., which have been woven since the Heian period, are among those shrine treasures. The pair of *Ueno-Hakama*-trousers introduced here is made of solid-twill with a design of camellia, and the *Akome* wear is made of double-fold fabric with a design of butterflies in circles over the background pattern of smal hollyhocks.

113
Katasuso Kosode Dress with
Design of Spring Plants and
Paulownia Flowers.

Embroidery and gold foils on *Nerinuki*
white silk.
Length: 119.0cm, Sleeve length: 49.5cm.
Momoyama period, 16th century.
Ura shrine, Kyoto.
Important Cultural Property.

This *Kosode* dress has been kept in Ura shrine at the end of the Tango peninsula in the northern part of Kyoto prefecture as a dress of the fairy tale heroin Oto-hime in the Dragon Palace in the sea.

As the size is rather small, this dress is considered a young girl's dress. *Kosode* dresses with designs on the shoulder and skirt parts are called *Katasuso* (sholuder and skirt) *Kosode*, which were popular in the middle and early modern ages. In the case of this dress, *Suhama*-shaped areas at the shoulders and skirt are divided into *Katami-gawari* forms, in which paulownia flowers and spring plants are arranged. The embroidered design is cheerful, and the violets, dandelions, plum and cherry blossoms as well as the horsetails are lovely. Both the design and embroidery technique show the charcteristics of *Kosode* dresses in the Momoyama period.

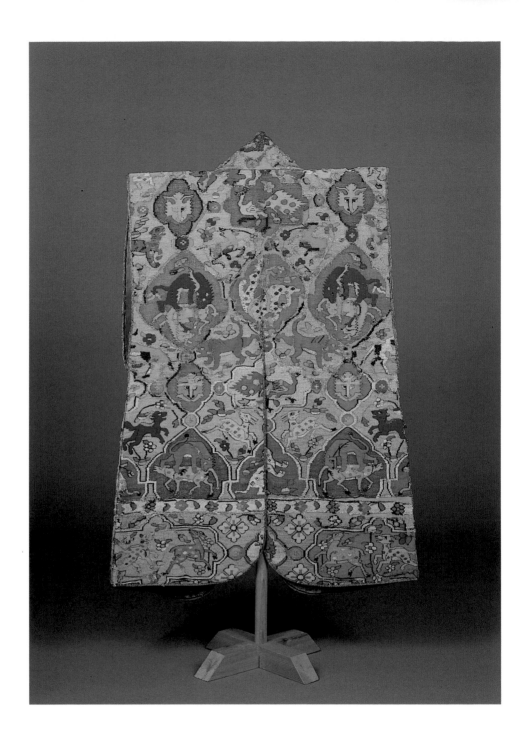

114
***Jimbaroi-vest with Design of
Birds and Animals.***

Brocade.
Length: 99.4cm, Width across shoulder:
59.4cm.
Momoyama period, 16th century.
Kōdai-ji temple, Kyoto.
Important Cultural Property.

This *Jimbaori*-vest, which was worn over the armor, was reportedly owned by Regent Toyotomi Hideyoshi. It has been kept in Kōdai-ji temple, which was founded by Hideyoshi's widow, Kita-no-mandokoro, for the commemoration of Hideyoshi.

Silk brocade was used for this vest. It is conceivable that this brocade was originally a rug made in Kashan in Persia. The design of a lion attacking his prey is one of the traditional motifs in Persian rugs. Persian rugs were imported to Japan by Portuguese ships, but because of the difference of life style, Japanese hardly used them as rugs. Toyotomi Hideyoshi, the high-spirited military officer in the Momoyama period, tried to create a gorgeous atmosphere even in the military camp by wearing a vest of arms made of an exotic rug.

115
Dōfuku-coat with Design of Cloves.

Nerinuki silk with tie-dyeing.
Length: 121.5cm, Sleeve length: 59.0cm.
Momoyama period, 17th century.
Kiyomizu-dera temple, Shimane.
Important Cultural Property.

This is a *Dōbuku* style coat with *Tsujigahana* tie-dyed design, which Shogun Tokugawa Ieyasu gave Yasuhara Dembei, a manager of the Iwami silver mine in 1603. Later, one of Dembei's descendants donated it to the local governor, and then the local governor donated it to Kiyomizu-dera temple, where it has been kept till now.

The design was dyed by using the so-called "Tsujigahana" method: large and small cloves are scattered in between the three horizontal zig-zag lines. The showing design with yellow and red as major colors reflects the taste of the Momoyama period. The technique of the tie-dyeing is elaborate, and even the narrow ends of the cloves were properly dyed.

This coat is an extant masterpiece with a clear historical background, and it shows an excellent design made during the period when the method of *Tsujigahana* tie-dyeing was most accomplished.

(detail)

116
Kake-fukusa Wrapper with Auspicious Design.

Satin, damask, and figured satin, and embroidery.
51.0 × 52.0cm.
Edo period, 17th century.
Kombu-in temple, Nara.
Important Cultural Property.

Thirty-one *Kake-fukusa* wrappers have been kept in Kombu-in temple in Nara. These wrappers together with gifts from the fifth Tokugawa Shogun Tsunayoshi were given to one of his mistresses, Zuishun-in. After Tsunayoshi's death, Zuishun-in donated them to Kombu-in temple for Tsunayoshi's memorial service.

These damask and figured satin wrappers are decorated with embroidered auspicious designs in colorful threads. The motifs are seasonal flowers, treasures, *Noshi*-ornaments, *Sake*-wine jars which are considered auspicious, and the Chinese characters "Fuku Ju", which indicate prosperity and longevity: All of these things are suitable for happy occasions. The embroidery was stitched with beautiful shiny silk threads, and sophisticated techniques were used, which make these wrappers refined pieces. These items are gorgeous *Kake-fukusa* wrappers of the Genroku era (17th century), which are noteworthy in the history of Japanese embroidery for showing the most elaborated embroidery technique of thoe days.

117
Furisode-dress with Design of
a Bundle of Noshi-ornaments.

Yūzen dyeing, tie-dyeing, embroidery
and gold-foil.
Length: 156.5cm, Sleeve length: 58.5cm.
Edo period, 18th century.
Yūzenshi-kai, Kyoto.
Important Cultural Property.

This is a representative _Yūzen_-dyed dress from the Edo period.
The designs of colorful _Noshi_-ornaments, which are bundled
at the left shoulder, are floating over the dress. First, red figured
crepe was tie-dyed, leaving the _Noshi_-ornaments section white.
Then, _Noshi-awabi_ strips were outlined by gold threads, and auspicious subjects such as a pine, bamboo, plum, paulownia, phoenix,
crane, peony, waves, _Shokkō_ pattern, etc. are arranged over
them. Various methods were used for these designs: _Yūzen-zome_
dyeing as the major method, embroidery, pressed gold-foil, and
Suribitta stencil dyeing, etc.

ROOM 15

The lacquer ware collection covers examples from the earlier pieces of the Heian period (10th century) to recent items of the late Edo and Meiji periods (19th century). It also contains Chinese and Korean lacquerware.

Lacquer is made of the sap of lacquer trees which grow only in Japan, Korea, China, and some South-East Asian countries, and therefore it is called an Oriental handicraft. Lacquer sap has a strong adhesiveness, and when it dries it becomes solid and the gloss of the surface stays permanently.

The main exhibits are *Maki'e* lacquered works. Design is made by gold or silver dust sprinkled onto a coat of still-wet lacquer, laid over the solid lacquer surface. This technique has been used since the Heian period for the decoration of stationery cases, toilet sets, ornaments, and tableware.

Lacquer sap which is originally transparent, turns red, black, yellow, and green through chemical processing. Lacquer ware of these four colors are also exhibited occasionally.

118
Maki'e Lacquered Box with Design of Hōsōge Flowers and Karyōbinga.

37.0 × 24.4 × 8.3cm.
Late Heian period, 10th century.
Ninna-ji temple, Kyoto.
National Treasure.

According to the two lines of the inscription on the lid, this box was made as a container for the Buddhist text *Sanjutchō-sasshi* which Priest Kūkai wrote in China and brought back to Japan during the Tang dynasty.

It is an oblong box with a lid of *Kabuse-futa* style. The box was first covered with cloth and then coated with many layers of black lacquer (*Sokusei* method). Gold and silver powder was sprinkled over the lacquered surface, over which *Hosoge* flowers, clouds, birds, butterflies, and *Karyōbinga* (imaginary birds in the paradise) are arranged symmetrically by using the *Togidashi Maki'e* technique. Each *Karyōbinga* is playing a musical instrument such as flute and drum, and the lively depiction of their motions is noteworthy.

According to the temple record, the Emperor gave this box to the temple as a container for the *Sanjutchō-sasshi*, when he read that text in the year 919.

119
***Maki'e Lacquered Sutra Case
with Design of Hōsōge Flowers
in Circles.***

20.3 × 33.0 × 17.0cm.
Late Heian period, 11th century.
Enryaku-ji temple, Shiga.
National Treasure.

The shapes of most of the extant sutra cases of the Heian period are oblong with slightly curved outlines and round corners, and *Kabuse-futa* style lids are attached. But unlike most cases, the outlines of the sutra case introduced in this article are straight and the corners are not round, and a lid of *Aikuchi* style, instead of *Kabuse-futa* style, is attached. These aspects reflect the characteristics of sutra cases made on the continent.

Eight circles are symmetrically arranged on the top and the sides of the case, and a *Hōsōge* flower with a diamond-shape in its center is shown within each circle. This symmetric design was made with the *Maki'e* technique, using gold, silver, and the mixture of gold and silver powder. Due to the density of the metalic powder, a slight variation is created. Is it conceivable that the *Hōsōge* flowers, which actually are a continental motif, were arranged in Japanese style for the decoration of this Buddhist utensil?

120
Maki'e Lacquered Hand-box
with Design of Sparrows.

27.4 × 41.2 × 19.1cm.
Late Heian period, 12th century.
Kongō-ji temple, Osaka.
Important Cultural Property.

This box has been called hand-box, although unlike other hand-boxes made during and after the Kamakura period, its lid is not in *Aikuchi* style but in *Kabuse-futa* style. It may be a hand-box of a classic style.

The entire body of the box is coated with black lacquer, and the *Togidashi Maki'e* method was used for the decoration of sparrows in the field. On a ridge there are millets and plantains. Some of the sparrows are flying, some are eating, and a sparrow hen is feeding her chicks. The back of the lid is decorated with plum blossoms in the manner of silver *Maki'e*. When considering these aspects one has to conclude that this hand-box was made in the late Heian period, when the motifs of *Maki'e* lacquered works were Japanized.

Accordiang to the inscription on the case of this hand-box, this hand-box was found in severely damaged condition by Mr. Tomio Yoshino when he was examining the temple properties at Kongō-ji temple in 1927; it was then repaired and kept in the temple.

121
Maki'e Lacquered Sutra Case with Design of Lotus Flowers.

32.5 × 20.9 × 20.0cm.
Kamakura period, 12th - 13th centuries.
Kanshū-ji temple, Kyoto.
Important Cultural Property.

Most of the sutra cases of the Kamakura period are decorated with illustrations of lotus ponds and lotus petals, and this sutra case is one of the typical examples.

This case is three-fold oblong. The top surface of the lid is slightly raised, and the corners are rounded. The entire case is coated with black lacquer. A lotus pond is described on the surface of the lid and the sides of the case, and there are scattered lotus petals. The method used for making this case is *Togidashi Maki'e*. Mainly gold powder was used, but some parts, such as waves are decorated with silver powder for variety. The inside of the lid and the case is also decorated with lotus petals. The metal fittings for the braids are attached to the lower part of the case. They are made of gilt bronze with open-work decorations of lotus flowers. All the decorations on this sutra case are lotus flowers. Thirteen volumes of the *Dainichi-kyō* sutra written in gold pigment on dark blue paper of this temple have been kept in this sutra case.

122
Maki'e Lacquered Hand-box
with Design of Nagi Trees.

25.5 × 34.2 × 22.3cm.
Muromachi period, 14th century.
Kumano Hayatama shrine, Wakayama.
National Treasure.

This is one of the twelve hand-boxes which have been kept in Kumano Hayatama shrine. It is said that those twelve boxes were donated separately by the Sentō Imperial Palace, the Muromachi Palace of the Shogun, and by government officials of several provinces.

These twelve hand-boxes can be classified into three groups according to the techniques used for their production, and into seven groups acccdording to the motifs of their decorations. It has been reportred that these twelve boxes represented twelve subsidiary shrines within the Kumano Hayatama shrine.

Nagi trees and rocks on a ridge are described both in the *Takamaki'e* method and inlaid mother-of-pearl on *Nashi-ji* lacquered surface. Cut gold and silver leaves were also used for accent. The same motif was used for the decorations on the surface of the box, inside of the lid, the two smaller *Kakego* cases, which are kept within the hand-box, and even on the cosmetic utensils. *Nagi* trees are holy trees of Kumano Hayatama shrine. This hand-box was donated to the Kanjō-gū subsidiary shrine within Kumano Hayatama shrine.

123
Red Lacquered Oshiki.

35.9 × 35.9 × 2.2cm,
36.7 × 36.7 × 2.3cm.
Muromachi period, dated 1457.
Masumida shrine, Aichi
Important Cultural Property.

Lacquered work of this kind is generally called "Negoro-nuri" ware of the Middle ages.

Masumida shrine was the foremost shrine in Owari (today's Aichi prefecture). Some pieces of *Oshiki* trays with rounded corners and some *Oshiki* of two different sizes with pointed corners have been kept in this shrine. The lacquered inscription of the name of this shrine is on the red lacquered surface, and the inscription of the date and the donor's name are on the black lacquered bottom of each object.

The shape of this ware is delicate and elegant, following the classic style of the Heian period, and the firm wooden frame does reflect the characteristics of the classic style, too. Solid layers of lacquer protect the wooden frame, and bright red lacquer was used for surface coating. Being excellent examples of lacquerware of this kind, all the *Oshiki* ware in Masumida shrine as a set have recently been registered as Important Cultural Properties.

124
Maki'e Lacquered Kasho
Chest with Design of Autumn
Plants.

22.0 × 31.5 × 38.0cm.
Momoyama period, 16th century.
Kōdai-ji temple, Kyoto.
Important Cultural Property.

The *Kōdai-ji Maki'e* method, which was used for this chest, was a representative lacquerwork technique in the Momoyama period. This chest is one of the most excellent extant *Kōdai-ji Maki'e* lacquered works.

Kasho chest is a container for the books and scrolls on the basic education for aristocrats; anthologies such as "Man'yō-shū", "Kokin Waka-shū", "Shin Kokin Waka-shū", etc., were kept in it. This chest has two rows of five drawers each, and the lid is in *kabuse-futa* style.

The entire body is coated with black lacquer, and the surfaces of the top and sides are decorated with autumn plants such as chrysanthemums, bush clovers, Japanese pampas grasses, pinks, and Chinese bell-flowers in the Gold-*hira-maki'e* method. It is amazing that even the sides of the drawers, which cannot be seen from the outside, are decorated with the same motifs.

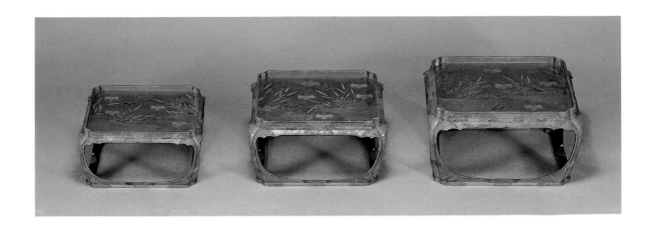

125
Maki'e Lacquered Tableware
with Design of Reeds.

Kakeban table: 33.5 × 34.5 × 17.7cm.
Momoyama period, 16th century.
Kōdai-ji temple, Kyoto.
Important Cultural Property.

This set of tableware has been kept in the Kōdai-ji Zen temple, which was founded by Regent Toyotomi Hideyoshi's wife, Kita-no-mandokoro, after Hideyoshi's death in 1606 for the purpose of Hideyoshi's commemorative service; it was her will to be buried there.

Three *Kakeban* tables in three sizes, a container for cooked rice and a rice server, and more than ten bowls in large and small sizes are in this set. All of them are decorated with streams, reeds, and paulownias in Gold-*hira-maki'e* over *Nashiji* lacquered surfaces, and the fittings are either in gold or silver. This set of gorgeous tableware was probably used by Regent Hideyoshi and his wife. Although this set of *Maki'e* lacquerware has been kept in Kōdai-ji temple, the manufacturing method was not *Kōdai-ji-maki'e* but a traditional *Maki'e* method.

126
Tsuishu Lacquered Tray with Design of Camellia and Blue Magpie.

Diameter: 32.4cm, Height: 3.5cm.
Yuan dynasty, 14th century.
Kōrin-in temple, Kyoto.
Important Cultural Property.

Tsuishu is lacquerwork with hundreds of solid layers of red lacquer and engraved decorations on the surface. It is an excellent Chinese technique which requires many hours of production.

Tsuishu engraved lacquerware was introduced to Japan together with Zen Buddhism during the Kamakura period and became inevitable for the Chinese style decorations of private libraries in the Muromachi period. Lacquered works made by this method were also used for the utensils for tea ceremonies. It can be said that *Tsuishu* became a representative lacquerware imported from China.

The entire surface of the top of this tray is decorated with camellias and a blue magpie. The tray is considered to have been made during the Yuan dynasty in China. The Chinese master craftman's name (Zhang Cheng) is engraved by needle on the back of the tray, but this inscription is assumed to have been added later in Japan. This inscription proves that the Japanese owners in the Muromachi period considered this tray as a most excellent piece of lacquerwork.

ROOM 16

The Kyoto National Museum keeps a wide variety of metalworks such as Buddhist implements, bronze mirrors, ornamental fittings, swords and armor.

Many of the Buddhist implements in our collection had been kept in temples in the Kyoto area; they include ritual tools and musical instruments, implements for Buddhist services, furniture and ornaments for temple halls, and several belongings of Buddhist priests.

Bronze mirrors were not always toilet utensils, but many of them were donations to temples and shrines. Mirrors made in Japan in the Chinese style, mirrors with casted decoration of original Japanese motifs, as well as Korean and Chinese mirros are among our mirror collection.

Our sword collection includes swords of both the old and new types. Old type swords were produced in Kyoto, Bizen (today's Okayama prefecture), Osaka, Yamato (today's Nara prefecture), Sagami (today's Kanagawa prefecture) and Mino (today's Gifu prefecture), where many talented swordsmiths were working during the middle ages. Some of the new type swords, which were made during the pre-modern ages, were made in large cities such as Kyoto, Osaka and Edo, whereas others were made in local provinces such as Hizen (today's Saga and Nagasaki prefectures) and Echizen (today's Fukui prefecture).

Our armor collection consists of *Ōyoroi* type armor-suits, which were in use between the late Heian and the Kamakura periods, *Dōmaru* type and *Haramaki* type armor-suits, which were in use during the Namboku-chō and Muromachi periods, and several protectors from the period of the civil wars and the Edo period.

The metalworks exhibits and exhibition theme are changed about once in every three months. Visitors watching the exhibits, can observe the techniques of molding, metal carving, and forging, as well as styles and designs of metalworks, and thus comprehend the history of Japanese handicraft techniques. The exhibition also conveys the tastes of people of ancient times, who appreciated these metalworks as part of the culture of those dys.

127
Gilt Bronze Gorin-tō Style
Cinerary Stupa for Buddha's
Relics

Total hight: 39.0cm.
Kamakura period, dated 1198.
Konomiya shrine, Shiga.
Important Cultural Property.

The worship of Shāka's (Sakyamuni's or Buddha's) relics began shortly after his death in India. Relics were usually kept in stupas in India, and they were traditionally kept within the foundations of stupas in Japan during the Asuka and Hakuhō periods. But since the Nara period, it had become common in Japan to keep relics within temple buildings and smaller cinerary stupas of various shapes have been made for that purpose.

This cinerary stupa contains a crystal cinerary container within its body. It was donated to Toshiman-ji temple in Ōmi (today's Shiga prefecture) by Priest Chōgen, who was promoting fundraising for the restoration of Tōdai-ji temple. Five components of *Gorin-tō* stupa symbolize five elements of the universe — earth, water, fire, wind, and sky. The characteristic aspect of this stupa is that the fire component is a trigonal pyramid. As cinerary stupas of the same style have been kept in Jōdo-ji temple in Harima (today's Hyōgo prefecture) and Amida-ji temple in Suō (today's Yamaguchi prefecture), both of which are related to Priest Chōgen, this style of stupa appears to have been invented by Chōgen.
(Inscription on the bottom)
    Donation to the *Hondō* Hall of Toshiman-ji temple in Ōmi.
    Gilt bronze Gorinto stupa, One item.
    Two pieces of relics.
    December, 1198.
    Donated by the Priest of Tōdai-ji temple.

129
Bronze Water Pitcher.

Height: 21.5cm, Body diameter: 10.8cm.
Kamakura period, dated 1276.
Shōjūraigō-ji temple, Shiga.
Important Cultural Property.

Water pitchers were originally used to keep drinking water in temples for the monks, but during the ancient times and middle ages water pitchers were often used as a Buddhist ritual implement to serve Buddha with purified water.

This water pitcher was made of bronze, and the body and the neck parts were smoothened by lathing. A spout and a lotus seat were jointed to the body, and the bottom plate was mounted at last. This water pitcher is noteworthy for its decorativeness with its spout in the shape of a dragon neck, the decoration of lotus with eight petals and the lotus seat.

It is known from the engraved inscription at the bottom that this pitcher was one of a pair of pitchers used for the *Fusatsu-e* ritual, when monks recite Buddhist precepts and make confession. Sansei-ji temple mentioned in the inscription is one of the *Tatchū* subsidiary temples within the Tōfuku-ji temple compound.
(Insecription)
    Bosatsu Kaini ...
    A pair of pitchers.
    Fusatsu ritual at Sansei-ji temple.
    August 1, 1276.

128
Bronze Waniguchi-Gong.

Diameter: 54.0cm, Thickness: 23.3cm.
Kamakura period, dated 1273.
Saikyō-ji temple, Shiga.
Important Cultural Property.

A *Waniguchi*-gong is hung from a temple's or shrine's eaves together with a rope to which a weight is attached at the height of the gong. Visitors are supposed to shake the hanging rope so that the attached weight will hit the gong before their prayers. The name "Waniguchi" (alligator mouth) is said to have come from the shape of the opening of the gong, which looks like an alligator's mouth. This name began to be used during the 15th century; before that, it was called "Kane-guchi" (metallic mouth), "Kane-tsuzumi" (metallic gong), or "Uchi-kane" (hitting metal).

This Waniguchi-gong is made of gilt bronze and the raised central part on its side is the place where the joint of the molds was during molding. The front and back surfaces of the body are raised higher than the surfaces of older gongs and pairs of lines divide the surface into four sections. The central part of the body, "Tsukiza", which is the place to be hit, is decorated with a molded design of a lotus flower with eight petals. The handles whose cross-sections are square were casted in one single mold. Below the handles, there are "eyes", but they hardly stand out from the surface. An engraved inscription is on the lower half of the gong's side. This is a typical *Waniguchi*-gong of the Kamakura period bearing the date of production.

(Inscription)
Kaneguchi of Jōfuku-ji temple, October, 1273.

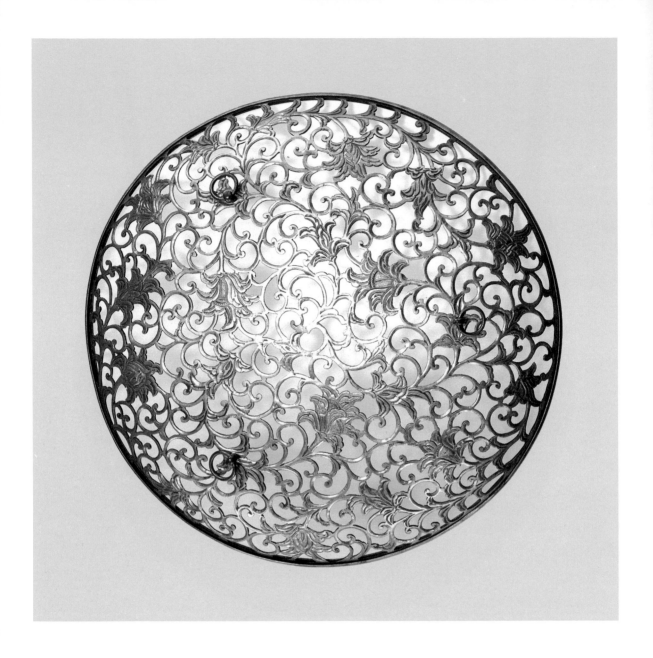

130
Gold and Silver Plated Keko
Ritual Basket with Openwork
Design of *Hōsōge* Flowers.

Diameter: 28.5cm.
Heian - Kamakura periods, 12th - 13th
centuries.
Jinshō-ji temple, Shiga.
National Treasure.

During some Buddhist ritual services, priests scatter petals made of paper. *Keko* is a basket for those ritual paper petals. Judging from the extant *Keko* objects in the Shōsō-in treasurehouse, *Keko*-baskets were originally woven with bamboo. Since Heian period, *Keko*-baskets have become more decorative. The decoration of this *Keko*-basket is most excellent both in its design and its technique among the extant pieces. *Hōsōge* flowers and vines, expanding from the center in three different directions are engraved in open-work on the whole surface of the bronze round plate of this piece. The method of *Suki-bori* (plow carving) was used on the outer surface to create a three-dimentional effect. The centers of flowers are line-engraved. The entire basket was gilt and some important parts of the *Hōsōge* flowers and vines were plated in silver over the gold surface.

The sixteen *Keko*-baskets kept in Jinshō-ji temple can be classified into two groups due to their elaborateness. Five of them are thought to have been made in the late Heian period.

131
Gilt Bronze Keman with
Shuji Sanskrit Letter in
the Center.

39.4 × 42.4cm.
Kamakura period, 13th century.
Hyōzu shrine, Shiga.
Important Cultural Property.

Both the inside and outside of the *Butsuden* halls in Buddhist temples are decorated gorgeously in order to represent the *Jōdo* Paradise. *Keman*-ornaments used to be hung from horizontal wall-partitions (Nageshi) and pillars. Many of the *Keman* were fan-shaped plates with open-work designs of plants or animals, but this *Keman* is different. The outline of this *Keman* ornament is composed of lotus flowers depicted upside-down. This style follows the original style of *Keman* — a garland for decorating Buddha's statues, but there are only a few extant examples of this style. A boat-shaped halo is placed on a lotus seat in the center of this *Keman*, and a *Shuji* Sanskrit letter, which represents Dainichi-nyorai (Vairocana), is in front of the halo. Some art-historias think that this style of *Keman* was established under the influence of *Shuji Kake-botoke*. *Shuji Kake-botoke* were metal plaques, which were regarded as mirrors, and to which *Shuji* Sanskrit letters representing saints were affixed. Those plaques were objects of worship.

132
Gilt Bronze Sutra Case with
Open-work Design of Lotus
Flowers and Vines.

30.5 × 19.1 × 10.4cm.
Muromachi period, dated 1555.
Yōhō-ji temple, Kyoto.
Important Cultural Property.

Buddhist sutras, which are the collection of Buddha's preachings, have been called "Hō-shari" and, together with "Busshari" (Buddha's relics), they have been treated as objects of worship. Therefore cases for keeping sutras have been made with various solemn decorations. Among them are many excellent pieces containing *Hokokyō* sutra scrolls: the faith in the *Hokekyō* sutra had become popular since the Heian period.

This sutra case is made of four bronze plates: the lid consists of two plates — one for the top and one for the sides, and the body also consists of two plates — one for the sides and one for the bottom. The joint between lid and body is rimmed with *Fukurin* decorations. The top and all the sides are decorated with lotuses and vines in openwork carving, and additonal *Sukibori* (plow-carving) of the details of petals and leaves have the decorations rise from the background. All the surfaces are gilt. But it is certain that the inscription on the bottom was engraved before gilting, which means that the inscription was engraved when the case was made. From that inscription it is known that this sutra case was made when a *Hokekyō* sutra was donated to Yōhō-ji temple.
(Inscription)
This object is to be kept in Yōhō-ji temple.
Donation, one copy of *Hokekyō* sutra in gold pigment on dark blue paper.
May 28, 1555.
Donor, Narita Yosaemon-no-jo Nagahiro.

133
Mirror with Design of a Plum Tree, Pheasants, and Sparrows.

Diameter: 24.7cm,
Height of the rim: 0.64cm.
Heian - Kamakura periods,
12th - 13th centuries.
Honnō-ji temple, Kyoto.
Important Cultural Property.

This mirror may have been donated in the donor's hope that his (or her) prayer be answered. The date of donation is unknown. This is a nickel mirror which consists of copper and a relatively large share of tin. The body is thick and large. The decoration on the back is as follows: A large sand bank is described at the bottom. There are rocks and streams in and in front of the sand bank. A pine tree on the sand bank is growing upward toward the left-hand side, and its trunk is described with emphasized outlines. Two pheasants and many birds, which look like sparrows, are flying.

The motifs were described on the mold, which was made of fine-grained clay, by impression with a comb-like metal tool. Originally, the decorations on the mirror-back were divided into two sections by a circle in the center — one section within the circle and one without it. But in the late Heian period people began to describe flowers and birds realistically on mirror-backs without dividing the surface into two sections; this style gained popularity between the late Heian and the Kamakura periods.

A mirror with a design quite similar to this one was excavated together with a cylindrical sutra case from the late 12th century from the sutra mound in Yamada Kyō-zuka of Baba in Gifu prefecture. The expression of trees on the mirror introduced here is slightly newer than the expression of trees on the Yamada Kyō-zuka mirror, but the shapes of rims and knobs are the same and both of the mirrors are large-size with diameters of more than 20 centimeters. All these aspects indicate that there is a high possibility of both mirrors coming from the same workshop.

134
Dōmaru-style Armor with Dark Blue Lacing, Helmet, and Ōsode-arm-protectors.

Height of the body: 33.9cm, Length of *Kusazuri*-skirt: 28.8cm, Height of the helmet: 10.8cm, Length of the *Ōsode*-protector: 36.4cm.
Muromachi period, 16th century.
Kenkun shrine, Kyoto.
Important Cultural Property.

Dōmaru-style armor used to be worn by foot soldiers. This style of armor encircles the soldier's body with the edges fastened together on the right side of the body. It was easy to wear, and its *Kusazuri*-skirt part was divided into more than five pieces to allow free movement of legs and hip. In these respects, *Dōmaru*-style armor was different from *Ōyoroi*-style armor for officers. But later, officers began to wear *Dōmaru* style armor as well and *Ōsode* (arm-protector) and helmets came to be used together with *Dōmaru*-style armor.

Some parts of the armor were formed by repetitively lacing together one small iron scale and two black lacquered leather scales. The lacing method used for this armor is "Kebiki-odoshi" using dark blue threads. The *Yonjukken Sujikabuto*-style helmet is made of forty iron plates, which are jointed together and coated with black lacquer. A *Kuwagata-dai*, which is gilt and bears an engraved design of chrysanthemums over its *Nanako-ji* texture, is fixed to the visor. *Kuwagata* horn-like gilt ornaments, and black lacquered and partly gold-foiled *Maetatemono* ornaments with a design of Chinese bell-flowers are attached to the *Kuwagata-dai*.

This armor shows several aspects of a classic style armor, but its *Kusazuri*-skirt part, which is divided into twelve pieces, and the small *Shikoro* (neck protectors) reflect the characteristics of armor of the late Muromachi period.

135
Dōmaru-style Armor with Silver
Scales and White Lacing, and
Gusoku-protectors.

Height of the body: 36.9cm,
Length of the skirt: 27.2cm,
Height of the helmet: 34.8cm.
Momoyama period, 16th century.
Itsukushima shrine, Hiroshima.
Important Cultural Property.

A set of protectors called "Tōsei-gusoku" (modern protectors) became fashionable between the end of the Muromachi period and the Momoyama period. "Tōsei-gusoku" protectors consisted of a helmet and a cheek-protector, which were made without the restrictions deriving from the fixed style of armor of the old days, and *Kote* (lower-arm protectors), *Haidate* (thigh protectors), and *Suneate* (leg protectors).

The helmet introduced in this article is unique. It has an *Eboshi*-hat-shaped ornament fixed over the iron helmet. This ornament was made of lacquered layers of paper and was decorated with silver foils and two black lacquered lines. Peacock feathers were sewn onto the neck protector of the helmet.

This *Dōmaru*-style armor is formed with silver-foiled small scales which are laced with white threads. *Mimi-ito* threads of the *Kusazuri*-skirt part and the *Ōsode* protectors for upper arms are not white but bluish yellow in order to create a contrast. The *Munaita*, which is the front part of the body, is decorated with a Gold-*maki'e* design of chrysanthemums and paulownias on the Silver-*nashi-ji* lacquered surface. The appearance of this armor with *Ōsode* protectors generally does not differ from *Dōmaru*-style armor-suits of the Muromachi period, but it has several characteristic aspects of armor made in the Momoyama period, such as small *Munaita*, rather round *Susoita*-plates of the *Kusazuri*-skirt, and design of paulownias on the major fittings.

LIST OF PLATES

ROOM 1

1 **Bronze Sword with a Hilt.**
Middle Yayoi period, 1st century B.C.

2 **Dōtaku Bronze Bell with a Tossen Type Handle and Kesa-dasuki Pattern.**
Late Yayoi period, 3rd century A.D.

ROOM 2

3 **Reliquary and Ornaments.**
Asuka period, late 7th century.

4 **Gilt-bronze Memorial Tablet of Ono-no-Emishi.**
Nara period, early 8th century.

5 **Tile with Design of an Angel.**
Asuka period, late 7th century.

6 **Gilt-bronze Cinerary Container for Ina-no-Ōmura's Ash.**
Asuka period, dated 707

7 **Gilt-bronze Cylindrical Sutra Case of Fuji-wara Michinaga.**
Late Heian period, dated 1007.

8 **Gilt-bronze Sutra Case.**
Late Heian period, 11th century.

9 **Mirror with Line-engraved Amitabha Triad and Twelve Buddhist Figures.**
Late Heian period, 11th century.

10 **Small Bronze Pagoda**
Late Heian period, 12th century.

ROOM 3

11 **Celadon and White Porcelain Containers of the Gosu Type.**
Esshū (Yue-zhou) kiln and Northern kiln in China.
Tang dynasty, 9th century.

12 **Temmoku Type Tea Bowl with Furnace-Transmuted Glazing.**
Ken (Jian) kiln in China.
Southern Song dynasty, 12th–13th centuries.

13 **Yuteki Mottled Temmoku Type Tea Bowl.**
Kaijin (Huai-ren) kiln in China.
Adjunct: *Temmoku* stand with mother-of-pearl inlaid decoration of arabesque vines.
Southern Song dynasty, 12th–13th centuries.

14 **Bluish White Porcelain Sake Bottle with Engraved Design of Clouds.**
Southern Song dynasty, 13th century.

15 **Celadon Bottle in the Shape of a Gourd with Patched Decoration of Peonies and Arabesque Vines.**
Appellation: "Gankai".
Ryūsen (Long-quan) kiln in China.
Southern Song–Yuan dynasties, 13th–14th centuries.

16-1 **Vases in the Son Shape with Five-colored Decorations of Dragons, Clouds, and Flowers.**
Inscription: "Produced during the Wan-li era in the Ming dynasty".
Keitokuchin (Jing-de-zhen) kiln.
Ming dynasty, 16th–17th centuries.

16-2 **Porcelain Case (Incense Burner) with Five-Colored Decorations of Lotus Flowers, Vines, and Dragons.**
Inscription: "Produced during the Wan-li era in the Ming dynasty".
Keitokuchin (Jing-de-zhen) kiln.
Ming dynasty, 16th–17th centuries.

17 **Purple Clay Water Pitcher.**
Gikou (Yixing) kiln.
Ming dynasty, 16th–17th centuries.

ROOM 4

18 **Ash-glazed Jar with Four Legs.**
Sanage kiln
Late Heian period, 10th century.

19 **Temmoku type Seto Porcelain Round Ink-stone.**
Seto kiln
Muromachi period, 15th century.

20 **Iga Ware Flower Vase.**
Known as "Ogura Iga".
Momoyama period, 16th century.

21 **Kokiyomizu Type Incense Burner in the Shape of Lotus with Polychrome Overglaze Painting.**
Attributed to Nonomura Ninsei.
Edo period, 17th century.

22 **Tea Bowl with Sabi'e Lacquered Decoration of Narcissi.**
Bearing the seal of Ninsei.
Edo period, 17th century.

23 **Gosu-Akae-utsushi Type Porcelain Dish with Decoration of Four Deities and Twelve Horary Animals.**
By Okuda Eisen.
Edo period, 18th century.

ROOM 5·6·7

24 **Seated Statue of Yakushi-nyorai (Bhaiṣajyaguru-tathāgata).**
Nara period, 8th century.

25 **Statue of Tamon-ten (Vaiśravaṇa).**
Late Heian period, 11th century.

26 **Wood-carved Ryōgai Mandalas.**
Late Heian period, 12th century.

27 **Standing Statue of Bishamon-ten (Vaiśravaṇa).**
Late Heian period, 12th century.

94 **Record of the Kanjō Baptism.**
By Priest Kūkai.
Early Heian period, 9th century.

95 **Calligraphic Volume.**
By Fujiwara Yukinari.
Late Heian period, 11th century.

96 **Kokin Waka-shū Anthology of Poems.**
Late Heian period, 12th century.

97 **Hokekyō Sutra in Gold on Purple Paper.**
Late Heian period, 12th century.

98 **Nihon Ryōi-ki.**
Late Heian period, 12th century.

99 **Certificate "Fuhō-jō,,**
By Priest Shunjō
Kamakura period, dated 1227.

100 **Ex-Emperor Go-Toba's Autograph Will with His Hand-prints.**
Kamakura period, dated 1239.

101 **Emperor Go-Uda's Autograph Will with His Hand-prints.**
Kamakura period, 14th century.

102 **Calligraphy by Priest Daitō-kokushi.**
Buddhist lesson to Sōgo Daishi.
Kamakura period, dated 1330.

103 **Calligraphy by Priest Jikusen Bonsen.**
Shozanso Greetings to Priest Meisō Seitetsu.
Namboku-chō period, 14th century.

104 **Risshō Ankoku-ron.**
Duplicated by Hon'ami Kōetsu.
Momoyama period, dated 1619.

105 **Bosatsu Shotai-kyō Sutra.**
West Wei dynasty, dated 550.

106 **Kongō-kyō (Vajra-sutra).**
Duplicated by Zhang Ji-zhi.
Southern Song dynasty, dated 1253.

107 **Calligraphic Frames and Plates for Zen Temples.**
Southern Song dynasty, 13th century.

108 **Calligraphy by Priest Gu-lin Qing-mao. "Getsurin".**
Yuan dynasty, dated 1327.

ROOM 14

109 **Kenda-kokushi Kesa-robe.**
Tang dynasty, 8th century.

110 **Shichijō Shinō Kesa-robe.**
Tang dynasty, 8th century.

111 **Ōhi-robe with Sammen-hōju and Katsuma Design.**
Kamakura period, 13th century.

112 **Akome Wear with Designs of Small Holly-hocks, Butterflies and Circles. Ueno-Hakama-trousers with Designs of Camellia and Vines.**
Namboku-chō period, ca. 1390.

113 **Katasuso Kosode Dress with Design of Spring Plants and Paulowniā Flowers.**
Momoyama period, 16th century.

114 **Jimbaroi-vest with Design of Birds and Animals.**
Momoyama period, 16th century.

115 **Dōfuku-coat with Design of Cloves.**
Momoyama period, 17th century.

116 **Kake-fukusa Wrapper with Auspicious Design.**
Edo period, 17th century.

117 **Furisode-dress with Design of a Bundle of Noshi-ornaments.**
Edo period, 18th century.

ROOM 15

118 **Maki'e Lacquered Box with Design of Hōsōge Flowers and Karyōbinga.**
Late Heian period, 10th century.

119 **Maki'e Lacquered Sutra Case with Design of Hōsōge Flowers in Circles.**
Late Heian period, 11th century.

120 **Maki'e Lacquered Hand-box with Design of Sparrows.**
Late Heian period, 12th century.

121 **Maki'e Lacquered Sutra Case with Design of Lotus Flowers.**
Kamakura period, 12th - 13th centuries.

122 **Maki'e Lacquered Hand-box with Design of Nagi Trees.**
Muromachi period, 14th century.

123 **Red Lacquered Oshiki.**
Muromachi period, dated 1457.

124 **Maki'e Lacquered Kasho Chest with Design of Autumn Plants.**
Momoyama period, 16th century.

125 **Maki'e Lacquered Tableware with Design of Reeds.**
Momoyama period, 16th century.

126 **Tsuishu Lacquered Tray with Design of Camellia and Blue Magpie.**
Yuan dynasty, 14th century.

ROOM 16

127 **Gilt Bronze Gorin-tō Style Cinerary Stupa for Buddha's Relics**
Kamakura period, dated 1198.

128 **Bronze Waniguchi-Gong.**
Kamakura period, dated 1273.

129 **Bronze Water Pitcher.**
Kamakura period, dated 1276.

130 **Gold and Silver Plated Keko Ritual Basket with Openwork Design of Hōsōge Flowers.**
Heian - Kamakura periods, 12th - 13th centuries.

131 **Gilt Bronze Keman with Shuji Sanskrit Letter in the Center.**
Kamakura period, 13th century.

132 **Gilt Bronze Sutra Case with Open-work Design of Lotus Flowers and Vines.**
Muromachi period, dated 1555.

133 **Mirror with Design of a Plum Tree, Pheasants, and Sparrows.**
Heian - Kamakura periods, 12th - 13th centuries.

134 **Dōmaru-style Armor with Dark Blue Lacing, Helmet, and Ōsode-arm-protectors.**
Muromachi period, 16th century.

135 **Dōmaru-style Armor with Silver Scales and White Lacing, and Gusoku-protectors.**
Momoyama period, 16th century.